Praise for *Love Hacks*

"Kelli Miller nails it! She has her finger on the pulse of what couples need to make things better quickly! She targets the main issues and gives user-friendly solutions for couples to get back on track. Thank you, Kelli, for this great piece of work!"
— **Dr. Debra Mandel**, author of *Sassy and Rude: Her New Attitude*

"This book brings real expertise to bear on one of the most important topics most people face, how to have a healthy relationship. It does so by always getting to the point in a remarkably readable and engaging way. It is sure to enrich the lives of everyone who reads it."
— **Steven Sloman**, coauthor of *The Knowledge Illusion*

"Since we get the largest portion of our happiness from our closest relationships, it's so worth our time and effort to learn how to make them great. Bravo to Kelli Miller, who offers us practical wisdom for growing fulfilling relationships."
— **Linda Bloom**, coauthor of *An End to Arguing: 101 Valuable Lessons for All Relationships*

"In this fast-paced, go-go-go world, couples need quick solutions to restore happiness to their relationship when tempers rise and disappointment reigns. Expert Kelli Miller offers quick, bite-size nuggets of wisdom to regain connection and love. A must-have for keeping the peace."
— **Arielle Ford**, author of *The Soulmate Secret*

"This book is precisely timed! With all the recent, unexpected strains at so many levels, Kelli Miller's *Love Hacks* is necessary for recapturing and rebuilding the foundation of a caring, safe, loving relationship no matter what the outside world brings."
— **Dave Pelzer**, *New York Times* bestselling author of *A Child Called "It"*

"*Love Hacks* is a must-read for anyone who wants to have a successful, fulfilling relationship! It's packed with smart, easy-to-follow, simple hacks to strengthen any bond."
— **Lyssie Lakatos, RDN, CDN, CFT**, and **Tammy Lakatos Shames, RDN, CDN, CFT**, authors of *The Nutrition Twins' Veggie Cure*

"*Love Hacks: Simple Solutions to Your Most Common Relationship Issues* lives up to its title. Psychotherapist and radio personality Kelli Miller has taken her years of personal and therapeutic wisdom and created a truly user-friendly guide for modern couples. I love how practical, actionable, and completely relatable it is, with wonderful stories from her actual clients that we can easily map ourselves onto. This book is a must-read for anyone who dreams of having a thriving intimate relationship."
— **Kelly Sullivan Walden**, bestselling author of *A Crisis Is a Terrible Thing to Waste*

"Kelli Miller, author of the bestseller *Thriving with ADHD Workbook for Kids*, has turned her attention to love. This easy read translates the complexity of relationships using familiar and compelling examples and provides the reader with three tools they can implement the moment they finish each chapter. If this book has half the influence on relationships as her workbook has had on kids with ADHD, look ⌐ trusting world courtesy of *Love Hacks*."
— **Joseph Shrand, MD**, president ⸱ and chief medical off

"Relationships are fraught with challenges. Psychotherapist Kelli Miller identifies the most common issues that plague romantic partners and deftly deconstructs them to offer practical solutions that anyone can implement. Grounded in Kelli's extensive therapeutic experience, *Love Hacks* is a gem for anyone wanting to improve their relationship quality."

— **Kory Floyd, PhD**, author of *The Loneliness Cure*

"*Love Hacks* illuminates all the patterns and challenges that modern couples face and clearly demonstrates how to make fundamental change. Kelli Miller guides us through the biggest challenges of romantic partnerships with compassion and even levity. What's extraordinary about this book is that it takes challenges that can be so full of pain and effort and shows us how to fundamentally shift our relationships — and thus our lives — with heartening simplicity. It reminds us of what's most important in our marriages and how to get there swiftly."

— **Faith Salie**, author of *Approval Junkie*
and contributor to CBS's *Sunday Morning* and NPR's *Wait Wait...Don't Tell Me!*

"What makes Kelli Miller's relationship expertise so cogent isn't just her deep understanding of the human condition, but the tenderness with which she delivers the salient relationship solutions. Kelli's voice comes across as equal parts seasoned psychotherapist and close friend who patiently helps you understand and avoid the follies that have unraveled so many relationships. It's the kind of empathy we could all use more of, and it's a refreshing and comforting read that can improve relationships that are weak — and strong!"

— **Maddox**, author of *The Alphabet of Manliness*

"I would have titled this book 'Everything You Need to Know to Make Your Romantic Relationship Work Forever.' *Love Hacks* is a practical masterpiece in which Kelli Miller brilliantly distills all the tools and practices couples need to have a successful, loving relationship. Kelli clearly identifies the typical issues that couples encounter and provides effective solutions for overcoming these problems. I'm going to recommend *Love Hacks* to all my patients!"

— **Ira Israel**, author of *How to Survive Your Childhood Now That You're an Adult*

"With *Love Hacks*, Kelli Miller gets to the heart and soul of relationships. The book reads like an invaluable communications cheat sheet, and I will be returning to it again and again!"

— **Samantha Ettus**, author of *The Pie Life*

"*Love Hacks* is filled with practical, easy-to-use tips and tools for couples. Kelli Miller's organization of the fifteen most common issues couples face will make addressing them approachable for those who want to make significant changes in their relationship from home."

— **Dr. Jenn Mann**, author of *The Relationship Fix:*
Dr. Jenn's 6-Step Guide to Improving Communication, Connection & Intimacy

LOVE
HACKS

Also by Kelli Miller

Thriving with ADHD Workbook for Kids:
60 Fun Activities to Help Children Self-Regulate,
Focus, and Succeed

LOVE
HACKS

Simple Solutions to
Your Most Common
Relationship Issues

Kelli Miller, LCSW, MSW

New World Library
Novato, California

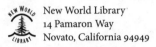

New World Library
14 Pamaron Way
Novato, California 94949

Illustrations on p. 60: From *The Happiness Hypothesis* by Jonathan Haidt, copyright © 2005. Reprinted by permission of Basic Books, an imprint of Hachette Book Group, Inc.

Text design by Tona Pearce Myers

Library of Congress Cataloging-in-Publication Data

Names: Miller, Kelli (Psychotherapist), author.
Title: Love hacks : simple solutions to your most common relationship issues / Kelli Miller, LCSW, MSW.
Description: Novato, California : New World Library, [2024] | Includes bibliographical references. | Summary: "An experienced therapist, radio personality, and bestselling author offers 21st-century solutions to the most frequent relationship pitfalls that continue to plague couples. In concise, easy-to-digest chapters, she breaks down the fifteen most common issues in relationships and provides three innovative solutions for each"-- Provided by publisher.
Identifiers: LCCN 2023048369 (print) | LCCN 2023048370 (ebook) | ISBN 9781608689088 (paperback) | ISBN 9781608689095 (epub)
Subjects: LCSH: Interpersonal relations. | Love--Psychological aspects.
Classification: LCC HM1106 .M535 2024 (print) | LCC HM1106 (ebook) | DDC 302--dc23/eng/20231106
LC record available at https://lccn.loc.gov/2023048369
LC ebook record available at https://lccn.loc.gov/2023048370

First printing, February 2024
ISBN 978-1-60868-908-8
Ebook ISBN 978-1-60868-909-5
Printed in Canada on 100% postconsumer-waste recycled paper

New World Library is proud to be a Gold Certified Environmentally Responsible Publisher. Publisher certification awarded by Green Press Initiative.

10   9   8   7   6   5   4   3   2   1

To Love: For those of us who are strong enough, wise enough, and brave enough to weather the storm.

Contents

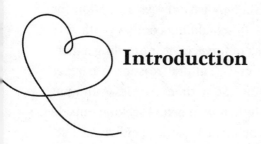 **Introduction**

Relationships are complicated. They are beautiful and messy and confusing and frustrating all at the same time. There are moments of joy, sadness, anger, uncertainty, and even boredom. All of this is normal and healthy.

Perhaps you've recognized that within these complicated relationships, certain issues arise over and over again. Do you find yourself having the same fight repeatedly? Are there a few issues that you and your partner just can't see eye to eye on? Is there one hot topic that you both avoid? Sometimes we need a little help navigating these issues. It's possible we have become too biased, too ingrained in our own feelings and emotions, and we need outside help to give us perspective. Regardless of what got us here, we choose to become brave and seek assistance.

As a psychotherapist, I've counseled thousands of couples, and I believe there is no substitute for couples therapy with a licensed therapist. Couples therapy is an interactive way to help partners establish goals within the relationship. The process is designed to help couples delve deeper into what is working and not working for them. It's a way for each partner to demonstrate their commitment to their relationship while gaining a better understanding of themselves and their partner. And it's especially necessary and helpful if there are more complex issues involved, such as trauma (sexual, emotional, verbal, and/or childhood), addiction, and/or a mental illness.

Unfortunately, couples therapy isn't always an option for everyone. This might be due to scheduling conflicts, difficulty balancing work and kids, lack of finances, fear of telling a therapist dark intimacies and secrets, cultural reasons, a partner who resists attending, and more. Sometimes couples even want to try to resolve problems on their own before seeking outside help. I wrote this book to help *any* couple who either can't attend couples therapy or wants to resolve issues on their own, perhaps as a supplement to therapy.

I've divided this book into the fifteen most-common issues couples experience, and for each issue, I provide three unique tools to help address them. *You can use any or all three of the tools; decide what you need and what works best for you.* I designed each tool to stand alone, and I tried to provide a variety of types and approaches. Some you may have heard of before, some maybe not, but *don't feel obligated to do all three every time.* My hope is that, even if one or two don't work for you, at least one will. Most exercises require just a pen and paper, and you might want to designate a specific journal for the work in this book. This way everything is in one place.

At times, the tools suggested may feel like work. That's because they are! I want to present no surprises. The exercises in this book require effort, dedication, and time, but the payoff of feeling more in sync with your partner is what makes it all worthwhile. If you have a moment of overwhelm while doing an exercise, it may be helpful to remember why you picked up the book in the first place. It's also wise to remember the only way for things to change is for things to change. That starts with doing things differently than you have been, which may involve talking or writing about hard topics and uncovering difficult truths. That being said, feel free to modify these exercises in whatever ways you wish. If something seems complicated or overwhelming, please simplify it. The point isn't to follow a set "program" but to discover and develop strategies that help you and your partner solve your particular issues together. Further, there is no need to proceed through the issues the way they are organized. You can start anywhere, with whatever issue is most important to you, and if you want, focus only on those issues that reflect your particular challenges. Later, if you recognize you have another issue, you can return to the book and use the tools for that particular issue.

Whether you are reading this book on your own or along with your partner, I hope it helps you gain insight into your relationship and provides concrete mechanisms for helping you improve and strengthen your relationship. Even if your partner is unavailable to read with you, I believe you can still gain powerful insight into yourself, a greater awareness of what you can change, a deeper education around communication and resolution, and a better understanding of relationships as a whole.

I'm glad you're taking the time to value yourself and your relationship. Rebuilding a relationship takes work. It can be eased, however, with four important hacks that exist within ourselves: being open, being patient, being the change agent, and being compassionate.

Being Open

Relationship work starts with being open — being open to learning and trying new ways. This involves recognizing old patterns that haven't been working and identifying new approaches that can make a difference. Openness means seeing our partner in a different light. It also means being willing to explore new and maybe unconventional techniques to seek understanding with our partner.

Being Patient

Relationship work also takes patience. This means being patient with both ourselves and our partner. We want others to be patient with us whenever we try new things, and our partners want that same grace. We need to be gentle with ourselves and our partner as we embark on this journey, knowing there may be some bumps along the way.

Being the Change Agent

We can only change ourselves, not other people. But if we focus on improving ourselves, on being a better partner for our partner, that solves at least 50 percent of the problem. "Being the change agent" means asking ourselves: Who do I want to be in this partnership regardless of my partner's actions?

Being Compassionate

Change doesn't take place overnight. Nor do improvements occur in a steady upward trajectory. We might move a few steps forward and then one step back. That's OK. We need to be compassionate with ourselves and our partner as we make efforts and occasionally stumble. Couples work is about progress, not perfection. What's important is continuing to try to improve our connection with our partner.

"My Partner Doesn't Listen to Me"

"**Y**ou never listen to me!"

"Hello, are you even hearing me?"

"I feel like the only time I'm heard is if *I scream*!"

One of the most satisfying parts of a relationship is feeling heard. It's sharing something vulnerable and feeling "seen," or completely understood, by our partner. Feeling seen is the ultimate indication of being valued, acknowledged, and appreciated. This means feeling like our partner understands what we've said and gets our wants, needs, and vulnerabilities.

Everyone wants to feel seen and heard. This is true across the board; we all want to feel appreciated and special. We all want to feel we matter. This is especially true in our relationships. Not only does listening well to our partner make them feel seen, but listening well prevents arguments. To be a better listener enables a deeper connection with our partner and ultimately a better partnership.

Listening is one of those concepts that seems simple in theory but is often difficult in practice. Many of us today may not even realize listening is a skill. In fact, we may never have been taught the skill of active listening nor even understand what true listening really means. For example, did you know that there is a distinct difference between "hearing" and "listening"?

Hearing is effortless, involuntary, and passive. We hear music and a dog barking down the street. We don't do anything to hear; sounds just reach our ears. Conversely, listening is focused and intentional; we are seeking information and understanding. We listen to our boss so we know what task they want us to do. We listen to directions. Listening is about processing communication, in part so we know what others want and what we should do, and this takes work and awareness.

If our partner ever says to us, "You're not listening to me," they aren't concerned that we haven't heard their words. Rather, they don't feel we are understanding their meaning, intentions, perspective, or emotions. They don't feel recognized or "seen." To put it another way, through active listening, we make our partner feel valued by seeking to understand them. In order to have a better partnership, we need to learn how to listen to each other, not just hear each other.

This chapter presents three listening tools: fast-food communication, "I" statements, and sounding board vs. feedback. Practicing these techniques with your partner will improve the quality of your listening and help your partner feel more connected and understood. These tools are essential for stronger communication and connection.

Fast-Food Communication

Conversations, requests, questions, and even comments from partners can easily get misheard and misinterpreted. It happens all the time, especially when partners are upset. This simple tool is useful for clarifying what someone has said.

In the multibillion-dollar fast-food industry, employees are trained to repeat each order when it's placed. For example, at McDonalds, if someone orders an Oreo McFlurry and a small fries, the employee will repeat back: "I have an Oreo McFlurry and a small fries." The order is also shown on the screen. That gives the customer the opportunity to correct the employee if they didn't hear the order correctly. This can happen easily for all sorts of reasons: It could be user error (the person didn't speak loudly enough or was indecisive and confused the employee), an equipment malfunction (the speaker wasn't working; the computer glitched), or general interference (kids screaming or someone else speaking). Accuracy is key, and repetition ensures clarity.

We can use this same technique with our partner and to serve the same purpose: to prevent miscommunication. Just like in fast-food restaurants, repeating what we hear gives our partner a chance to make sure we have heard them correctly. This technique also forces both partners to slow down, which helps keep emotions from taking over.

For instance, Milo and Talia, a couple in their thirties, came to me because they both felt they weren't "listening to each other." I asked for an example. Talia told me that just last night Milo had come home late from work, cooked, and then completely forgotten to clean up the dishes, which left a mess in the kitchen. Talia admitted that when she woke up in the morning and saw the mess, she "snapped" at Milo. Milo said he couldn't understand why Talia was so angry. Talia shrugged and said, "See, he just doesn't get it!"

I suggested that they both experiment with fast-food communication. To practice, I asked Talia to first say how *she* was feeling.

Talia: "I felt upset that you came home late, then didn't clean up the dishes."

Then I asked Milo to repeat back what he heard.

Milo: "What I'm hearing you say is that you felt upset that I came home late, then didn't clean up the dishes."

The phrase "What I'm hearing you say is ..." signals that Milo is confirming his understanding. This gives partners the opportunity to correct each other if they hear the statement wrong. It's a small but mighty phrase. First, Milo needs to make sure he is hearing exactly what Talia is trying to communicate.

This effort to confirm understanding, while providing the opportunity for clarification, helps partners feel heard. Once Milo repeated back what Talia said, she immediately felt understood and validated and was able to soften. Validation was the missing piece of the puzzle; suddenly, she felt like a priority because Milo was making her one. Milo still didn't understand why the dirty dishes made her so angry, but for Talia, it wasn't really about the mess. She wanted her feelings confirmed.

Our instinct is often to defend or protect ourselves. But once we feel validated, we can let our guard down. We can then be more receptive to our partner's experience or perspective.

Milo: "I'm so sorry I was late and didn't clean up the dishes. I can understand how that can feel frustrating, especially when you see it first thing in the morning. My supervisor had me finish up one last spreadsheet, and I was exhausted by the time I got home."

Milo took accountability and acknowledged Talia's feelings, and then he explained why it happened. This helped Talia let go of her anger, and she used the fast-food technique with Milo:

Talia: "What I'm hearing you say is that your supervisor kept you at work late, so you were too tired to clean up after the meal you made, and you're sorry about that. It was hard for me to see the mess in the morning, but I understand why it happened. I'm sorry I snapped at you. It was unnecessary."

In general, partners feel less defensive once they feel heard, first and foremost. Talia was angry, but once Milo validated her — simply by repeating her words using fast-food communication — she felt more connected and seen.

To clarify, fast-food communication just involves repeating back what a partner has said to ensure clarity and validate the partner. It's not about defending ourselves. The goal is to make our partner feel understood.

As Talia and Milo demonstrate, this is about more than merely repetition. Here is an initial template for this kind of conversation, which you can follow and adapt as needed:

Partner 1: I feel _____ [name feeling] about the _____ [circumstance].

Partner 2: What I'm hearing you say is that you feel _____ [name feeling] about the _____ [circumstance].

Partners then alternate "hearing" each other until both feel supported and understood. The conversation should end with apologies from both partners for their parts. Again, this is not a time to defend or prove your point; it's more about trying to confirm your partner's feelings.

It can sound a bit odd at first to just repeat back what a partner is saying, and people may even feel a bit like a parrot. But active listening begins with making sure we hear our partner correctly and that they feel validated. It's as simple as starting with: "What I'm hearing you say is ..."

"I" Statements

There is simple communication. Then there is *strong* communication. As couples, we want to strive for strong communication. Think of the Olympics. We don't just want the bronze medal — we want the gold! Simple communication is like aiming for any medal, and strong communication is like aiming for the gold. Obviously, we want to strive for the gold or strong communication. Life stressors happen, and couples can get stuck in simple communication. This could mean haphazardly stating needs and frustrations without thinking about how they affect a partner. People aren't focused on tone or how a partner is receiving or listening to their messages. People can get lost in their own needs. Instead, we can avoid this by focusing on strong communication using "I" statements.

"I" statements are a style of communication that focuses on naming the feelings or reactions of the speaker rather than judging the actions and intentions of the listener. This means the speaker first takes responsibility for their reaction, rather than blaming the partner for whatever they did that upset the speaker. If a partner forgot date night, for example, an "I" statement would sound like, "I feel angry you forgot our date night."

In contrast, "you" messages are the exact opposite of "I" statements; they focus on what the other person has done. In the same example, a "you" message might sound like, "You are so self-centered and once again forgot our date night!"

Unfortunately, most people tend to use "you" messages because they get caught up in their own emotions. We have to remember that the words we use will have a direct impact on how our partners react. Listen to how much kinder an "I" message sounds if our partner forgets the milk:

"You" message: "You are so irresponsible! You always forget the milk!"

"I" statement: "I feel frustrated when you forget to pick up the items I asked for at the grocery store."

Dana and Christina were high school sweethearts. They met as teens and felt they never developed a mature way to speak to one another. They were still interacting like fifteen-year-olds when they were in their midforties. The two immediately started arguing in my office, and I heard several "you" messages.

> **Dana:** "You are always on your phone! You never pay attention to me!"

> **Christina:** "That's because you're always yelling at me! Plus you're on your phone, too!"

Dana blamed Christina for what she was doing, and not doing, using a "you" message, but Dana didn't actually say how she felt.

Christina immediately felt attacked and angry with Dana's tone, and so she defended herself by blaming Dana using her own "you" message. If Dana had expressed how she felt first, Christina might have felt empathy for Dana, but since Dana didn't, Christina just told Dana what she felt Dana was doing wrong. After being criticized, Christina became defensive and unable to imagine or relate to what Dana was feeling.

In truth, Dana felt hurt and wanted Christina to pay more attention to her. But instead of being vulnerable and communicating that she felt hurt, she became angry and accusatory. Dana may have had a right to feel upset or hurt, but she needed to use an "I" statement to state her needs in a way that would elicit a better and more empathetic response from Christina.

I asked the women to start the conversation over using "I" statements. First, I asked Dana what she felt when Christina was on the phone.

"I feel ignored," she said. "And sad."

"OK," I said. "This time, using an 'I' message, tell Christina what you're feeling."

Dana: "I feel sad that you're on your phone often. It makes me feel like you don't want to be with me."

Dana did more than describe her own hurt feelings. She explained why they arose, out of her own insecurity. This openness and vulnerability changed Christina's reaction.

Christina: "I'm so sorry. I didn't realize I was on my phone that much. I do want to be with you."

This is the power of "I" statements and why they are like "going for the gold." Christina heard Dana's hurt and felt badly, and she immediately reassured her. The real problem wasn't actually what Christina was doing, but how Dana interpreted and felt about it.

When partners use "you" messages, they instantly feel protective. When partners use "I" messages, they become open and receptive, which helps foster empathy.

In essence, an "I" message always starts with "I feel..." Then it states what the feeling is a reaction to, but without blaming the other person: "I feel _____ when _____ happens."

Using "I" statements takes practice. Use them in everyday life, and you will find that people are generally more receptive to what you are saying. It's gentler on the ears. Using them forces us to really think about what we're feeling and what we need in that moment. It forces us to slow down.

"I" messages are a considerate way to express how we feel without placing blame on a partner, and they are an effective way to avoid further conflict.

Sounding Board vs. Feedback

What do you consider to be the qualities of a good listener? Is it someone who gives you eye contact, sits close, and doesn't interrupt when you are talking? Or is it someone who nods and acknowledges what you are describing by saying, "Yeah, I get it," "That must be so hard," or "How can I help?"

In fact, these represent two different types of listening using two types of communication: nonverbal and verbal.

Nonverbal communication conveys information without words. It includes eye contact, physical proximity, gestures, and facial expressions.

Verbal communication uses speech. Both types of communication are useful and valid, and we often use both together. But when it comes to listening, we tend to use nonverbal communication when we're being "sounding boards" and verbal communication when we are offering "feedback," and it's important to know which one a partner needs or prefers.

Couples come to me frustrated because they feel their partner isn't "listening" to them. What is interesting is that their partner often looks baffled and confused when they hear this. The partner assures me that they are genuinely listening. And they are. In *their* mind.

The confusion or disagreement often lies in the type of listening. If one person wants a sounding board, which stresses nonverbal communication, and the other person is offering feedback, which requires verbal communication, then the partner who is sharing isn't getting the kind of listening they want. So the key is determining and asking for the communication style a partner prefers.

Being a sounding board essentially means listening to a partner without commenting, offering advice, or trying to fix a problem. Being a sounding board sounds easy, right? In practice, it's not always easy. In fact, it's hard to only listen and not respond, especially if our partner is struggling with an issue. We want to jump in and help. Someone describes their problem and we want to rescue them. Some people assume or have been taught that active listening is supposed to include giving feedback or advice.

The truth is, sometimes people don't want to be rescued, and getting unsolicited feedback can sometimes make them feel even worse. They may feel like they are not doing enough or doing the wrong thing. Sometimes people just want to vent without comments. They need a literal sounding board. In this case, all a partner wants is nonverbal communication: for their partner to sit with them face to face, give eye contact, and nod to acknowledge that they are listening and sympathetic. Being heard is enough.

On the other hand, at times, people genuinely do want feedback. They want their partner to reflect, comment, empathize, share their perspective, and help them brainstorm solutions. They don't want their partner to sit quietly. They want them to say things like, "I get how that can be frustrating," "How can I help you with this?" and "Do you want to come up with ideas together?"

How do partners get what they want or provide the type of listening that helps someone best? We simply ask. Oftentimes, partners can't understand why their needs aren't being met. For example, a partner may feel worse after they vent, even getting angry and frustrated, because getting feedback from their partner, whatever the advice, makes them feel not good enough. What the partner wanted was a sounding board, but since they didn't ask for that, the other partner didn't know. The partner who is listening is trying to be helpful by offering feedback, but when that makes their partner feel worse, they now feel worse, too, even purposeless. Their intention is to be helpful, but they haven't given what their partner needs. These types of situations can be avoided if a partner expresses what type of listening they need from the start, or if the person listening asks what their partner prefers.

We aren't mind readers. We need to effectively communicate our needs in order to get those needs met. Nor should we assume what someone else wants. People might feel shy about telling a partner how to listen, to either be a sounding board or give feedback. But remember, partners want to help and want to know the best way to provide that help. Giving direction, and asking for direction, helps both partners. The person listening wants to feel good knowing they helped in the way their partner needed.

So when your partner wants to talk, ask them: "Would you like me to be a sounding board or do you want feedback?" You can ask this after they finish speaking and before jumping in with advice, just to confirm. Alternatively, if you want to share with your partner, before telling your story, tell them how you want them to listen: "Can you please just be a sounding board right now?" Or, "I really need your feedback." With direction, partners have a blueprint for how to listen most effectively.

By using all three of these techniques — fast-food communication, "I" statements, and sounding board vs. feedback listening — we can listen better, help understand and validate our partners, and ultimately form deeper connections.

ISSUE 2

"We Are Constantly Arguing!"

You love your partner. You care for your partner. Yet you can't stop arguing with them. It doesn't matter whether the squabble is small or large. You argue over something simple like who did (or *did not*) put the dishes away or something more complicated like if your partner exchanged numbers with an attractive somebody at the neighbor party last week. Either way, you just can't stop arguing. At times you may even question if you should still be together.

Conflict is a healthy and natural part of any relationship. All couples argue at some point. What matters most is how couples handle and resolve those conflicts.

When conflicts are handled in a respectful and productive manner, it can build trust in the partnership. After working through arguments, couples can feel more closely connected because honesty, authenticity, and understanding are brought to the table. Partners are able to see the other's point of view. When we learn to argue in a healthy manner, future arguments cause less anxiety and are often resolved more productively, with more compromise.

The three techniques this chapter explores for helping you resolve arguments in healthy ways include using time-outs, using a scaling system to understand who is more emotionally invested, and assuming positive intentions. But before diving into the tools, it's important to examine the first thing we need to do: gain control over our own anger.

Anger is a natural emotion, but if not channeled correctly, it can be very damaging. Once partners learn how to manage their anger better, they tend to argue less as a couple.

When we get angry, our brains go into overdrive. We get so wrapped up in feeling hurt or frustrated that we can't communicate kindly or even think rationally. We become single-mindedly focused on getting our point across. Consequently, others may not be able to hear what we are trying to say because their defenses go up, especially if we are loud and/or yelling. This can create a negative cycle. One partner gets angry, the other partner gets defensive, neither partner hears the other, and both end up frustrated. Each time, the dynamic repeats.

It's important to break this cycle.

Communication is a two-way street. That means recognizing it's not enough to just want to feel heard; partners must be receptive to what the other is saying. For example, if one person is screaming, their partner might stop trying to listen at all, and they won't be able to listen as well to the other's point of view. In an argument, we need to learn not only to listen better but how to communicate in healthier ways. That starts with acknowledging our own anger so we don't yell, slam doors, make sarcastic or snide comments, and more.

Recognizing when we become angry comes more easily for some than others. If you have trouble sensing when you become angry, pay attention to body cues, since anger starts physically. Often, when people become angry, their heart races, their palms get sweaty, their face turns red, they speak quickly and/or loudly, they fidget, or they clench their fists. Some get headaches or stomachaches, become quiet, or shut down. Everyone's reaction to anger is different, and the goal is to become aware of your signals when you're angry so you can address your feelings before they escalate and reach a damaging level. For more about anger, see also Issue 15: "There Is Too Much Anger Between Us" (page 171).

Think of anger on a scale from 1 to 10: 1 is totally calm, and 10 is feeling out of control. The key is to pause any conversation or argument when we reach about a 6 out of 10 on the scale. Pausing is simple but not easy. Pausing involves recognizing we're losing control of our emotions and stopping a conversation, or whatever is happening, then stepping aside to do whatever is necessary to calm down before resuming. This is what a time-out is for, which I discuss next. The key is to acknowledge we're getting angry, the conversation is getting heated, and we need a separation from the discussion. What people consider their "level 6" will differ, but to me, it means still being able to converse without yelling or screaming.

Some people think that pausing at level 6 isn't necessary, since they still feel somewhat in control, but anger can escalate quickly. Once we're at a level 6, it can only take a few exchanges to shoot right up to a 10. The point of pausing is to prevent escalation, so it's better to pause "too soon" than too late.

Time-Outs

Most people associate time-outs with childhood. For some parents, it can be a standard punishment for a mischievous child, who is forced to sit in a corner to reflect on what they did. In school, teachers sometimes use time-outs to manage unruly kids, but being punished in front of a classroom, or in front of anyone, can cause feelings of shame. Most of us associate time-outs with painful experiences and bad behavior.

That's not what this time-out is about. Contrary to childhood time-outs, this relationship-focused time-out is meant to be restorative, not punitive. In other words, this time-out is not a disciplinary action but an investment in the relationship. It's a mature way for either or both parties to take a breather. It's a pause to allow our brains and bodies to calm down so we can hear each other. It's a way of letting go in the present for the sake of having a more fruitful outcome in the future.

However, the first step for implementing time-outs successfully is establishing the rules with a partner beforehand. This should be done when you and your partner are calm, collected, and not in the middle of an active argument. Here are what I consider the five basic rules for time-outs:

Rules for Time-Outs

1. Time-outs can be requested by either person, but they should be asked for calmly.

2. Both partners agree to respect the other's request for a time-out. That means stopping the argument or conversation immediately. It may be tempting to continue talking or to get the last word in, but it's imperative that when the time-out is requested, both partners agree to stop talking.

3. Both partners agree to a certain length for a time-out, meaning that they set a time limit for coming back to the conversation. Time-outs are not a means to end a discussion; they are a break from a conversation so one or both partners can calm down. Usually, two hours is a good length, though partners can convene sooner or later if they both agree.

4. The person who calls the time-out is the person in charge of reconvening the conversation after the time-out, or they can ask for more time if needed.

5. There are no limits to the number of time-outs. Either partner can ask for as many time-outs as needed within the same conversation.

Using Time-Outs

If you recognize that you're angry, and have reached level 6 or above, pause the conversation and ask your partner for a time-out. If you recognize that your partner is angry, it's also OK to ask for a time-out on behalf of both of you. It's not about who asks for the time-out. If either person is heated, the couple needs a time-out.

Here is an example of how to ask for a time-out:

I can see that we are both getting heated and I want to ask for a time-out. I think it will be good for both of us to pause and calm down. Let's meet back here in two hours.

During the time-out, do whatever helps you to get calm. That can include things like taking a walk, listening to calming music, journaling, doing push-ups or exercise, calling a friend, or watching TV. If possible, get some distance from your partner. If distance is not possible, focus on your preferred activity as best you can. The most important thing is stopping the conversation in order to prevent further damage.

Then when the time-out is over, the person who called the time-out is in charge of reconvening the conversation. If conversation again causes an escalation of emotion, it's OK to take another time-out and repeat.

Often, schedules, kids, or other factors may delay the typical two-hour time limit. This may happen if an argument arises before bed or work. If so, the important thing is to communicate about when you plan to reconvene. For example, you might say:

It's very late. I suggest we take a time-out until tomorrow morning at 9 a.m. after we drop off the kids at school. Can we finish our discussion then?

Time-outs are a very effective way to prevent an argument from escalating further. They may be hard to implement at first, but with practice, they become easier. Pausing gives partners the opportunity to slow down and reflect and prevent strong emotion from harming a relationship.

Who Is More Emotionally Invested?

Arguments take many forms. Sometimes an argument can feel big to one partner and small to the other. I've found it helpful for couples to recognize who is more emotionally invested in, or feels more strongly about, an issue or outcome, and I developed a simple tool that helps them figure out the relative importance to each person.

Like self-evaluating the level of anger, this involves rating the level of emotional investment in the outcome on a scale from 1 to 10: 1 equals barely any investment, and 10 is a very strong investment.

Here is a hypothetical example: Saturday night is date night for Alana and Boris. Alana feels strongly about seeing a certain movie that she missed seeing the previous week. Boris wants to watch a live sports game. As they discuss what to do, they each start getting frustrated, since the other won't budge from their choice. Before the discussion becomes an argument, they ask each other: "On a scale from one to ten, how emotionally invested are you in your choice?" Alana says, "I'm a seven out of ten for the movie because we didn't get to see this movie on our last date night." Boris says, "I'm a five out of ten because I just went to a game last weekend with a friend."

The agreement is that the person who is more invested gets their choice. In this scenario, that would be Alana because she is more invested in the movie than Boris is in his game.

Of course, this technique only works if both partners are

truthful and honest about their self-evaluation. Ideally, part of being in a partnership is committing to honesty. However, the technique tends to even out. When partners are flexible when their emotional investment is low, that encourages flexibility in the other when their emotional investment is low. When partners are honest, it's rare that one partner is always more invested and so gets their choice almost every time.

If both partners are exactly equal in emotional investment, they might simply flip a coin to determine the final choice. That's a simple way to assure fairness and equality.

Using the emotional investment scale works on more complicated issues as well. For example, Sean and Rick were a loving couple in their fifties who couldn't agree on household tasks. Sean had a pretty large wardrobe and did laundry once a month for the two of them. Rick was more of a once-a-week laundry guy. Rick was getting frustrated because he wanted to do the laundry every week. I asked the couple to rate their emotional investment.

Rick reported he was a 9. He claimed he had "a bit of OCD" and didn't like the smell of dirty clothes. He couldn't understand how someone wouldn't want clean, fresh clothes.

Sean was more nonchalant about the issue, but quantifying the relative importance of the issue helped them resolve it. He said, "You know, I am probably a five. Clearly, I don't love doing laundry or need to do it very often. But I recognize it's more difficult for Rick with the smell factor than it is for me. So he gets this one. We will do it once a week."

Using this simple scale is a way to be relatively objective with yourself about your preferences. Then, when comparing it to your partner's investment, it's often clear what the outcome should be. Use this technique proactively to prevent an argument from escalating.

Assuming Positive Intentions

An important step to creating a more cohesive relationship is for partners to assume positive intentions. That means giving our partners the benefit of the doubt. Partners are in the relationship together. They are a unit. A team. A relationship isn't a competition where one individual wins first place at being best in relationships. Partners win together when they strive to be the best couple they can be.

Assuming positive intentions is a mindset shift. It's about reframing our thoughts.

When we get frustrated with our partner, we can sometimes feel like they are intentionally doing something to annoy us or deliberately disregarding our feelings. The majority of the time, we are all just trying to do the best we can, but we can get so focused on our own point of view that we forget our partner's point of view. Assuming positive intentions is a way to remind ourselves that our partners love and care for us, even if or when they do something that upsets us. Their goal isn't to hurt us. In fact, it's the opposite. Our partner's goal is generally positive; they want us to be happy. Thus, assuming positive intentions is a way to foster compassion for our partner, and at minimum give them the benefit of the doubt, so we can take a more objective step back and find a compromise or solution.

In the heat of the moment, though, it can be a struggle to assume positive intentions. Here are a few techniques to try:

1. Put yourself in your partner's shoes. Why do you think they feel the way they do? What are they hoping to get out of the discussion?
2. Do you feel your partner did anything on purpose? If so, what and why exactly?

3. If assuming positive intentions doesn't feel possible, can you assume neutral intentions? In other words, can you view their intentions as neither positive nor negative?

4. Think back to why you fell in love with your partner in the first place. Was it their kindness, intelligence, humor? When we first fall in love, we typically assume positive intentions, so recalling that can help. For more on this, see Issue 5: "I Don't Feel in Love with My Partner Anymore" (page 57).

5. Consider if you have any underlying resentments you're carrying. Resentments can cloud us from regarding our partner in an unbiased way. For more on dealing with resentments, see "Looking at Resentments" (page 40).

Assuming positive intentions is a great tool to remind ourselves that we and our partner are a team achieving the same goal. We need to assume positive intentions from our partner in order to gain a greater perspective and have a better relationship.

Arguing is normal in relationships. Partners won't always be able to see the other's point of view. Sometimes our own feelings get the best of us. However, by using time-outs to help manage anger, evaluating who is more emotionally invested in the outcome, and assuming positive intentions, we will get along better as a couple.

ISSUE 3

"We Don't Make Time for Each Other"

One of the common complaints I hear from clients is how their partner doesn't have time for them anymore. "They are always at work!" is a big one, as is "The kids just take up all our time together." People sometimes defend not making more time for their partner by saying, "I finally get a chance to be by myself!" or "I need to take care of my aging mother." While all these reasons may be legit, the problem remains. Partners aren't spending enough time together and it's affecting their relationship.

The initial phase of dating and courtship is fun. Everything feels light and easy. Partners prioritize each other, sometimes above everything and everyone else. Further, in general, the younger people are, the fewer responsibilities and the more freedom they have, so it can be easier "back then" to arrange plenty of uninterrupted time with a partner. That's how we build our initial connection.

The solution to this relationship problem is obvious: We need to make our partner a priority. That is how we rebuild a connection that feels lacking. Prioritizing a partner takes effort by both people, and at times, one partner might not feel like making the effort. My antidote to this is: *Don't wait for the feeling, take action.*

People often wait for inspiration to take action. This may even be unconscious. When we feel happy, we go to the party.

When we feel motivated, we go to the gym. Conversely, if we don't feel happy, we skip the party. If we feel sluggish and tired, we put off the gym. We mean to, we know we should socialize or exercise, but if we never feel like it, we never do. Our plans never happen.

So turn this around, especially when it comes to rebuilding a relationship. Take action first, which can lead to or inspire the feeling. Go to the party, and socializing will inspire happiness. Go to the gym, and exercising will fire up motivation. Make time for your partner, and this will help you both feel more closely connected.

The three tactics for prioritizing your partner are date nights, quick partner connections, and exploring the resistance. Apply all three in order to help put your partner first.

Date Nights and Scheduling

One surefire way to prioritize your partner is to schedule date nights. What works best is to schedule a consistent date once a week. Dates can be day or evening, but set aside at least one to two hours of uninterrupted time with your partner. If once a week is too much for either partner's schedule, then do it twice a month. The important thing is to plan: Set aside a specific time beforehand, commit to that time, and follow through.

It's helpful to treat the date like any other important appointment. That's what it means to prioritize a partner. Don't cancel or postpone the date unless there is a genuinely critical conflict or a true emergency.

When it comes to logistics, it's easiest to agree on the same day and time each week. This way, both partners can plan ahead and work other things in their schedule around their regular date night. For example, make date night a repeated event in a shared calendar.

Often couples tell me it's too hard to find the time for a date night. So I remind them: Our actions convey our priorities. When something is important, we make time for it, and vice versa. If you recognize how important this time is for your partner, you will see the importance of setting a time. Of course, our lives are full. Finding time is not always easy. But there is always a way. If evenings are too difficult, maybe a regular breakfast or lunch would work. The day and the time don't matter. Even what you do doesn't really matter. What matters is taking time to prioritize your relationship.

If one person is more committed to creating a date night, but the other isn't, talk about it. A simple conversation can make a big difference. Here is one way to approach that conversation:

> *I really value our relationship and would love to create a deeper connection. I know we are both busy and it's difficult to find the time, but I would like to prioritize our relationship so we can feel more connected. Although it might be hard to find the time initially, I know once we carve it out, it will be a really wonderful experience for both of us.*

Another issue can be who takes responsibility for planning. A fair approach so that neither partner feels pressured is to alternate who makes the plans. Each week (or every other week) one partner plans the date, deciding the setting and the activity, and next time, the other partner takes over. This way, partners not only share the responsibility, but they each have a chance to plan things they enjoy.

What should you do on these dates? The intention is to bring some lightness back into your relationship and to have fun with each other! Dates are not a time to have hard conversations about difficult topics. Use this time to let go and be free within your relationship.

Couples sometimes struggle with inspiration for what to do on a date. I always suggest thinking about what people did when they were first dating. Did they love ice skating? The movies? Taking walks in nature?

Here is a list of ideas to consider:

- Eat at a new restaurant, and go to a different one for dessert
- Cook a new recipe together
- Get some color-by-number kits and paint together, or go to a painting event like Paint n' Sip or Color Me Mine
- Play a sport together like tennis or riding bikes
- Have a spa night and purchase low-cost face masks
- Make a picnic lunch or dinner in the park
- Take a dance class together
- Attend a live performance, like a concert or a comedy show
- Go fruit picking
- Do an adventurous activity like rock climbing
- Go to a water park or theme park
- Tour a winery or brewery
- Go ax throwing
- Make your own pizza
- Go to an arcade
- Surprise each other by ordering a partner's favorite ice cream
- Go bowling

If money is a concern, plenty of options are low or no cost:

- Walk around the neighborhood or explore a new neighborhood

- Have a board game night
- Volunteer together at a soup kitchen or other charity venue
- Hike together
- Go camping and build a campfire
- Watch the sunset or sunrise
- Take a drive and listen to music or an audiobook
- Play hide and seek
- Read to each other (perhaps a steamy romance novel!)
- Create a scavenger hunt
- Sleep late and have breakfast in bed
- Do couples yoga
- Look at the stars
- Visit a dog park or animal sanctuary
- Listen to a lecture at a local library or college

Remember, the point isn't the amount of money couples spend. Rather, date night is about partners giving each other their undivided attention and having fun together!

Finally, when couples have children, that adds another complication to arranging a date night. Be creative here as well. If a couple can't afford a babysitter, maybe they can offer to swap babysitting with friends who also have kids; that way, both couples can have a date night. Another option is that some gyms and other venues (like IKEA) offer on-site childcare, which might allow a couple to be together while their child is supervised safely. Alternatively, a couple could bring their child with them to a local park: While their child plays on the playground, the couple can sit on a bench. Local community centers also offer programs, like sports or crafts for kids, and a couple could plan their dates for when their child is doing a program. Another option is to schedule a date night at home when kids are asleep or even early in the morning before they wake up. The essential point is for partners to set aside time for each other.

Quick Partner Connections

Date nights are very important. Equally important is for partners to make smaller, simpler, quicker connections during the course of a normal, busy day. A "quick partner connection" is exactly what it sounds like.

When partners have been together a long time, everyday responsibilities and conversation can hold major weight: "Did you put away the laundry?" "What should we do for dinner tonight?" "Remember that Jack has soccer practice at 4:30." Of course, it's necessary to communicate about everyday logistics, but it's just as important to make room for fun little connections in a relationship.

I like to divide quick partner connections into five categories that I term TEASE: traditions, efforts, acknowledgments, silly, and erotic. Each category is different and a valuable way to connect when partners don't have a lot of time.

Traditions

Traditions between you and your partner are important in a relationship. They allow couples to feel connected by having something just for *them*. Think about simple rituals you could add to your relationship. Perhaps you could create a morning gratitude ritual; each day you would tell each other the five things you're grateful for. This would start your day on a positive note, and studies show making a gratitude list can make people happier. Alternatively, make a tradition of taking a morning or evening walk together. Make a ritual out of having coffee or tea together for ten minutes before going to work. A tradition can be as simple as kissing your partner goodbye before leaving in the morning and kissing them hello when you return. The focus here is establishing a habit or ritual that is just between the two of you.

Efforts

Part of being a good partner is helping your partner. A powerful way to connect is by helping your partner in some quick, everyday way. Some examples are scraping ice off the car windshield in winter, picking up groceries for dinner that night, or tidying up the house.

Acknowledgments

As I discuss in the first chapter, we all want to feel seen, heard, and acknowledged. One great way to make a quick partner connection is to do something to make our partner feel valued. We could handwrite our partner a note before they leave for work, which is always a fun surprise. This could be a simple expression of appreciation, like, "You mean so much to me," or "I really value how much you do for me." Alternatively, partners can tell each other something they love about the other: "I love that when you laugh, your nose crinkles." A gesture like a hug can let our partner know how much they mean to us. Acknowledgments are a beautiful way to connect with our partner.

On the other hand, if you yourself don't feel acknowledged by your partner, remember that positive behavior toward a partner begets positive behavior. In other words, if we give, we're more likely to get.

Silly

We often forget that silliness in a relationship is not only necessary but super helpful in connecting. Commit to being silly with your partner once a day. What's the worst that could happen? Talk in a foreign accent, wrestle with each other, or make silly faces before going to bed. Laughter is healing and a wonderful way to connect. If this is hard for you, perhaps it's something to strive for: Use this strategy to break free of feeling the need to be serious and responsible 24/7. Silliness can remind our partners that we are multifaceted humans and that our relationship can be funny, too.

Erotic

Another way we can connect with our partner quickly is in an erotic way. This doesn't mean necessarily having sex, though it could. The idea is to supplement regular sexual connection. For instance, a quick flirty text can go a long way to putting a partner in a good mood. Perhaps send your partner a steamy text first thing in the morning while they are on their way to work. Alternatively, write and send a sweet poem or sensual quote. Remember, sex doesn't always start in the bedroom! These hacks could be a fun way to entice and excite your partner in a spontaneous way. It's also fun to be sensual outside of everyday responsibilities. It reminds us that we're in a healthy sexual relationship.

Whichever quick partner connection you decide to try, I suggest putting a reminder in your calendar. Every day, remind yourself to quickly connect with your partner in some capacity using TEASE. Do only one thing — say, be silly by putting on a pig nose before coming home from work — or alternate between all five. A little effort goes a long way toward fostering connection and feeling closer with our partners.

Exploring the Resistance

When clients avoid something, there is typically a deeper reason underneath. So when partners aren't choosing to make time for each other, they need to explore what is behind the resistance, reluctance, or lack of effort.

For example, Jenny and Stefan were two kind and loving thirty-year-olds. Jenny desperately wanted to spend more time with Stefan but would often stop herself from doing so. One week Jenny came to our session and talked about her goals: She wanted to say yes to dates with Stefan, have more intimate conversations with him, and have more physical touch. We set up a schedule and structure for doing these things. But despite being genuinely motivated, Jenny didn't follow through. The next week, she came to our session and told me she hadn't said yes to any dates with Stefan, failed in having more intimate conversations with him, and denied having more physical touch.

So we explored this resistance, and eventually, after several sessions, Jenny felt safe enough to admit that she had been sexually abused as a child. Even though she desperately wanted to spend more time with Stefan, it was terrifying to her. Remaining aloof meant no one could hurt her, physically or emotionally. This reaction, and her resistance to spending more time with Stefan, was understandable, given her trauma, but Jenny also wanted to overcome her fear. After long and hard work on Jenny's part, we processed her trauma together, and Jenny was able to start spending more time with Stefan.

If you and your partner are hesitant to spend more time together, explore this resistance. Ask yourself and each other what reason either of you may have for not wanting to spend more time together.

Here are three common issues along with solutions for addressing them:

Fear of intimacy: Is it a fear of intimacy? Could it be fear that if you are emotionally close that carries the expectation of physically intimacy? Are you afraid that, if you spend time together, you will have to talk about certain topics that one or both of you don't feel like answering?

One way to address this is to tell your partner exactly what you want. Set specific boundaries and expectations. For example, you might say, "I want to spend the day with you, but right now I'm not ready to be physically intimate. Is it OK if we just spend the day together with no pressure to have sex afterward?" Make sure to ask your partner if they agree with your request. Or you might say, "I am really excited to go on a road trip with you. Is it OK if we don't talk about my mother on this trip? That topic upsets me and I want to have fun with you."

Ongoing frustrations: Consider if there is something your partner is doing that frustrates or bothers you. Are there issues or behaviors causing ongoing irritations, particularly anything that you haven't voiced before and that your partner might not be aware of?

If you recognize a habit that you don't like, address it directly and, if appropriate, ask your partner to stop. For instance: "I am really looking forward to our road trip, but can you please put your phone away while driving? When you focus on your phone, I get anxious and don't feel safe, and it gets in the way of enjoying your company." Or if you sense that your partner is frustrated, ask them directly, "Is there something that I do that bothers you that I may not be aware of?" The answer might be hard to hear, but it could also be something that you never knew upset your partner, and now you can clear the air and start spending more time together.

Lingering resentments: Are you holding on to any resentments with your partner? Do you think they are holding a grudge about something you have done?

Resentments toward a partner usually relate to some hurt in the past that a partner can't let go of or forgive. Depending on what it is, if this is something you feel, can you recognize the source of resentment and decide now to practice forgiveness and let it go? Would you feel comfortable sharing your feelings with your partner? A partner might be unaware of resentments, they might feel their partner's anger but not know what it relates to, or they might know but be afraid to address it, express remorse, and ask for forgiveness. Obviously, this may involve a deeper conversation, and for more on addressing resentments, see "Looking at Resentments" (page 40).

These strategies — scheduling regular date nights, making quick partner connections, and exploring resistance — are ways to make our partner feel like a priority again. Some weeks you may be able to put in more effort than other weeks, and that's OK. Life is about achieving a successful balance. The key is for making time for your partner to become something you both do consistently.

"We Don't Have Sex Anymore"

One of the difficult topics for couples to talk about is the diminished desire for sex. The irony is that it's also one of the most common issues among couples. Since sex is uncomfortable for many people to discuss, it often becomes easier for partners to avoid each other than to bring it to the table. That's going to change starting today. We are going to bring the conversation of sex to the table.

Sex is an important part of a relationship. It's also the one factor that differentiates partnerships from friendships. Like any other aspect of relationships, sex involves emotional connection, trust in the partnership, communication, and more. And if the other parts of a relationship need improvement, a couple's sexual relationship often suffers and may need improvement, too. But if sex isn't discussed or closely examined, it can't be improved.

The question of sexual frequency is often the first issue that arises, but there is no "right" amount of sex. The right amount is what works best for both partners. Less sex doesn't mean a worse relationship and more sex doesn't equate to a better relationship. Since sex depends on or reflects a couple's emotional connection, the strength or weakness of that connection can drive each person's libido up or down.

It's important to note that even in a healthy relationship, sexual frequency will ebb and flow. Some weeks it will happen more often or more consistently, and other times it won't. The concern is when one or both partners is unhappy and experiencing a diminished desire for sex.

If you or your partner have a diminished sex drive, the first and most important step is to get a physical exam from a medical doctor. First rule out any medical issues. A hormone imbalance, physical issues, and even an addiction to drugs or alcohol can greatly affect a person's sex drive.

If there aren't any medical issues, look deeper into improving your sexual relationship. Here are three strategies to try: looking at resentments, sensate focus therapy, and setting the scene.

Looking at Resentments

Resentments arise when we feel we have been treated unfairly. People can carry resentments toward their partner that they are or aren't aware of, but any resentment will impact our emotional or sexual relationship. When people feel hurt by something their partner did, intentionally or unintentionally, they no longer feel safe to have sex with their partner.

Resentments can stem from many things: infidelity, frustration over doing more of the household chores, angry words, and so on. Resentments can be deep and long-lasting, and some brew over time. In any case, if resentments are blocking emotional and sexual connection, they need to be addressed.

By acknowledging and exploring the source of any resentments, we can take steps to let the resentments go. Letting go doesn't mean forgetting that the action happened or denying that hurt feelings are valid; it doesn't mean instantly forgiving a partner. It's recognizing that the resentment is no longer serving either partner and is causing damage to the relationship.

I recommend following these six steps for letting go of

resentments: (1) acknowledge your feelings, (2) identify why you feel resentful, (3) communicate with your partner, (4) state your needs, (5) forgive, and (6) look at your own expectations going forward. Here is more detail on each step:

1. Acknowledge Your Feelings

In order to start healing, we need to allow ourselves the permission to feel the emotions associated with the resentment. It's OK to be hurt, angry, confused, or sad about what happened. The important thing is to accept what we feel and no longer deny our emotions.

Write down your feelings in a sentence or two. This is a concrete way to acknowledge what you're experiencing. Here's an example: "I'm angry because my partner had photos of other women on his camera roll, and I feel sad and insecure because it makes me wonder if I'm enough."

2. Identify Why You Feel Resentful

Be specific about exactly why you feel resentful. Do you feel your partner doesn't understand your point of view? Do you feel misunderstood about your feelings? Do you feel your partner did something intentionally hurtful? Again, write this down: "I'm resentful that my partner initially denied having photos of women on his phone and I had to discover them myself. I'm also resentful because at first I questioned my own sanity and felt like maybe I was going crazy."

3. Communicate with Your Partner

It's important to discuss an ongoing resentment, even if it has been brought up before. Obviously, those previous discussions didn't resolve the issue. Make sure to use "I" statements (see page 9) when explaining how you feel and what you want. Here's an example: "I want to work on our relationship because I believe we have something good. I know we've talked about it before, but I recognize I'm carrying a resentment about the photos I saw on your phone. I still feel angry and sad about it. I'd like to continue this conversation so we can ultimately resolve it."

4. State Your Needs

Think about what you need from your partner. Do you need the opportunity to tell them you're still hurt? Do you need more explanation of what happened? Would you want an apology? If they already did apologize, do you need a more detailed apology? Describe what you need so your partner can understand how they can help you. For example: "I believe what would help me is a truthful apology. I am not sure I see complete remorse about what happened."

5. Forgive

Forgiveness is not always easy, but it is a powerful tool for letting go of resentment. Forgiving doesn't mean forgetting what happened or condoning hurtful behavior. It just means being ready to let go of feeling angry and hurt so you and your partner can move on. For example: "What happened hurt me a great deal. But I'm ready to forgive you and move on from this."

6. Look at Your Own Expectations Going Forward

Sometimes people hold on to resentment because they have certain expectations of how things should have been. It's important to let go of those expectations and accept things for what they are or were. That means stepping out of idealized hopes and honoring the reality of the situation. This might involve setting new boundaries. For example: "I know I've gotten angry with you before when you look at other women. I believe what can help us going forward is establishing boundaries around photos. We have never talked about what we are both comfortable with."

Remember, letting go of resentment is a process, not an event. That means it may take time to forgive or let go of any resentment. But be patient with yourself and your partner. Releasing a resentment can be a powerful and healing tool that restores sexuality in a relationship.

Sensate Focus Therapy

If partners aren't quite ready yet to resume sexual intercourse, I recommend trying sensate focus therapy as a starting point.

Sensate focus therapy is a technique created by Dr. Virginia Johnson and Dr. William Masters. It's used to improve intimacy and communication between partners around sex, and it focuses on touching and being touched. The technique consists of five steps that partners follow in a sequence. These steps help couples start the process of being sexually intimate again by taking the pressure off performance, orgasm, and any other sexual patterns that may have caused the couple stress.

This description of sensate focus therapy is based on Masters, Johnson, and Kolodny's book *Heterosexuality* as well as Cornell Health's pamphlet "Sensate Focus." Please note: Although Masters and Johnson's book is titled *Heterosexuality*, this technique applies to all sexual identities and orientations.

The five steps include (1) nongenital touching, (2) genital touching, (3) adding lotion, (4) mutual touching, and (5) sensual intercourse.

Before starting, it's important for both partners to adopt an open mind. Naturally, as people become intimate again, they may feel or fear being uncomfortable. So start this process by putting aside any preconceived notions or judgments around sex, sensuality, touch, personal preferences, and what is happening. This includes judgments like, "Do I like this touch?" "This is boring," and "Am I going to make my partner happy?" Judgments may arise, and that is OK. When they do, people should bring their focus back to the present moment and their sensations.

Next, focus on exploring sensuality rather than having sex. In other words, this process is about being aware of our bodies and exploring touch and being touched, not engaging in sexual acts. In fact, up until the final step, the intention is to avoid orgasm and intercourse, so partners should commit to each other to refrain from sex until that step, no matter how turned on they become. Denying sex is not a punishment. Rather, it's meant to help partners focus on discovery and sensation itself.

The process is intended to build slowly; each step is meant to take anywhere between twenty minutes and an hour, and only one step should be done at a time. Wait for the next or another day to proceed to the next step, and then only if both partners feel comfortable doing so. If one partner wants to repeat a step, keep doing so until both partners are ready to progress to the next step.

When partners are ready, choose a private area without distractions. Ideally, partners are undressed, but if one person doesn't feel comfortable, it's OK to do step 1 fully clothed or in undergarments. Here are details on each step:

Step 1: Nongenital Touching

Designate one partner to be the "toucher" and the other as the "receiver." Both partners will play both roles, so it doesn't matter who starts in which role. The receiving partner should focus on their own sensations, and they should not reciprocate the touch. The point is for the receiver to take in the sensations. The receiver should speak out if the toucher does something physically or emotionally uncomfortable.

Instructions:

1. Designate the initial "toucher" and "receiver."
2. Allow each person about ten to fifteen minutes in each role as toucher and receiver.
3. The toucher starts by caressing the parts of the receiver's body that are normally visible, such as hands, neck, feet, scalp, and face. The toucher can vary the tempo and firmness of touch. The toucher is looking for different textures, contours, and temperatures of the various body parts. If this step is done with clothes on, it's up to the recipient whether they want to be touched over or under their clothing.
4. When ready, the toucher moves to the back, arms, and legs.
5. Finally, the toucher moves to the chest, stomach, and shoulders, but avoiding the breast, buttocks, and groin areas.
6. The partners switch roles. The "toucher" now becomes the "receiver" and vice versa.
7. If either partner wants to stop at any stage, they are permitted to do so.

Many couples may do step 1 for several days before moving on. There is no time limit or "right" time to move on. Couples should only move to the next step when both feel comfortable.

Step 2: Genital Touching

Like step 1, genital touching is meant to be sensual, not sexual. The point is not to turn on a partner or to be turned on. The goal is tactile exploration of the whole body, but this time, it also includes the genital area, buttocks, and breasts. Refrain from kissing and intercourse in this exploration.

Instructions:

1. Designate the initial "toucher" and "receiver."
2. Allow each person about ten to fifteen minutes in each role as toucher and receiver.
3. The toucher starts by caressing all the parts of the body explored in step 1, while also moving to the breasts, groin, and all places. The toucher should continue to explore the whole body and not stay focused only on the breasts and groin area.
4. This time, the receiver may opt to place a hand on the toucher's hand as a guide to show how the receiver would like to be touched: firmer, softer, longer in certain places, and so on. The receiver is meant to occasionally guide touch, not to take over what the toucher does.
5. The partners switch roles. The "toucher" now becomes the "receiver" and vice versa.
6. If either partner becomes aroused, that is OK. If the receiver becomes aroused enough to orgasm, that is also OK. However, the goal is not to orgasm, and partners should refrain from kissing and intercourse.
7. If at any point either partner wants to stop, they are permitted to do so.

Step 3: Adding Lotion

In step 3, add lotion, and as in step 2, touch can include the entire body, including genitals and breasts. The idea is to focus on how the lotion feels different on the body and creates a more sensual experience. As in step 2, partners should refrain from kissing and intercourse. Almost any kind of lotion is fine, but I suggest using an alcohol-free, hypoallergenic lotion or lubricant.

Instructions:

1. Designate the initial "toucher" and "receiver."
2. Allow each person about ten to fifteen minutes in each role as toucher and receiver.
3. This time using lotion, the toucher caresses all parts of the body, and they again focus on the whole body, including the genital area and breasts but not exclusively. One suggestion is to begin touching without the lotion and then add it partway. Also, experiment by only using the lotion on one hand and not the other for contrast. As in step 3, the receiver may occasionally guide the toucher's hand.
4. The partners switch roles. The "toucher" now becomes the "receiver" and vice versa.
5. As in step 2, if either partner becomes aroused or orgasms, that is OK, but the goal is not to orgasm. Continue to refrain from kissing and intercourse.
6. If either partner wants to stop, they are permitted to do so.

Step 4: Mutual Touching

In step 4, both partners mutually touch each other at the same time. There is no longer a designated toucher or receiver. Both partners are invited to explore the other. With mutual touching, sensory feelings come from two places simultaneously — from touching the other and from being touched. The point is to shift focus between each source of stimulation until the two sensations naturally melt into a single, unified experience. If a person notices they're only focusing on one or the other, they should switch their attention to touching or being touched.

Instructions:

1. Both partners caress the other at the same time, with neither being a toucher or receiver. As in the previous steps, partners are naked and focus on the whole body, including genitals and breasts; they may use lotion if they want; and they can guide the touch of the other. Partners should shift their focus between both sources of sensation, touching and being touched.

2. Mutual touching can continue for any preestablished amount of time or as long as both partners want. Again, partners should focus on the sensual awareness they are feeling rather than the sexual experience.

3. As before, if partners become aroused or orgasm, that is OK, but the goal is not to excite or arouse the other to orgasm. Continue to refrain from kissing or intercourse.

4. If either partner wants to stop, they are permitted to do so.

Step 5: Sensual Intercourse

The final step of sensate focus therapy is to engage in sensual intercourse, not sexual intercourse. That is, the goal remains the same: to explore and experience sensation, slowly and with awareness, rather than to intentionally arouse the other in order to have an orgasm. Focus on what feels pleasurable and include all aspects of the previous steps.

Instructions:

1. Both partners start with mutual touching of the whole body. Proceed slowly and focus first on nongenital touching, and only gradually extend to breasts and

genitals. As in previous steps, partners are naked, can use lotion, and can guide their partner's hands.

2. Sensual intercourse can extend for a preestablished length of time or for as long as both partners want.

3. After mutual touching for a while, once both partners are ready, choose a position that allows for intercourse. At first, simply allow the genital areas to touch while partners continue touching each other with their hands. Go slowly and keep exploring the sensations actively.

4. If both want sensual intercourse, start with slow partial penetration. Hold absolutely still for a few seconds in between movements and focus on the sensations, such as warmth, contact, and so on.

5. Slowly withdraw for twenty to thirty seconds and then resume slow partial penetration.

6. If either partner wants to stop, they are permitted to do so.

Sensate focus therapy is a wonderful way to restore sensuality to sex, so we focus on touch and sensory input rather than the act of intercourse itself. Sensate focus therapy takes the pressure off sex as a performance. Rather, it is an exploratory encounter that helps us reconnect with our partner not just sexually but sensually.

Setting the Scene

Everyone has preferences. Consider how people work best at their jobs. Some people like to have absolute quiet so they can focus. Others like to have music on in the background. Some like to work late at night. Others like to take multiple breaks. What works best for each individual varies.

The same applies to sex. Physically and emotionally, every

person varies in what helps them feel the most safe and comfortable and in what they like and dislike. Using the red-light/green-light approach, we can identify and understand what feels good in our bodies as well as identify the environment that feels most comfortable, and then we can share that with our partner. That helps foster a more enjoyable and connective experience.

Green-Light and Red-Light Behaviors

People tend to make lots of assumptions about sexual preferences. People often think they know what their partner likes and wants in regard to sex, but that might not be true. Just because one person likes a certain touch doesn't mean a partner will also automatically like it. Alternatively, sometimes people are afraid to speak up and tell their partner what they do or don't like, leaving partners to make assumptions that are wrong. Further, sometimes partners get into sexual habits that get stale; both may want to try new things and be afraid to say so, assuming the other only likes the way it is. That's why it's essential for partners to have honest, open conversations about sex to prevent presumptions and lack of communication undermining sexual connection.

This strategy focuses on identifying what we like (green-light behaviors), what we don't like (red-light behaviors), and what environment we prefer (such as timing, venue, and so on). Initially, each partner writes in a journal and explores these things for themselves, then in a separate conversation, they describe and explain their personal preferences to their partner.

It's important to emphasize that this is not about judging the other person; it's not meant to criticize or blame. The goal isn't to tell the partner what they are doing wrong or accuse them of not being a good lover. That said, avoid the urge to appease the other by telling them only what they want to hear. In other words, the point is for partners to honestly express their sexual preferences without criticizing their partner or taking care of their feelings.

To be successful, both partners need to pledge not to take the other's likes and dislikes personally. The goal of the conversation is to establish a deeper connection and learn more about what delights and upsets the other, their affinity for touch. When partners can feel safe to talk about sex, they are already building a better sexual relationship.

GREEN-LIGHT BEHAVIORS

Green-light behaviors are what feel good physically, verbally, and emotionally in regard to foreplay and sex.

Explore this first on your own by writing in a journal; perhaps complete a chart like the one below. Starting with your head and working all the way down to your toes, what are the things that you love, physically, verbally, and emotionally?

Green-Light Behaviors		
Physical	*Verbal*	*Emotional*
I love kisses on my neck.	*I really like compliments during foreplay.*	*I like when my partner calls me throughout the day. It makes me feel connected to them after work.*
I love when my partner goes slow with his tongue up and down my body.	*I really like when my partner calls my name during intercourse.*	*I like when my partner tells me what they love about me.*

51

For example, physically, do you like kisses on your neck or to have your breasts caressed? What pressure or speed of touch do you like in specific areas? Consider any areas that aren't being touched as much as you prefer.

Verbally, do you like hearing compliments or sex talk? Do you like being told what turns your partner on? Do you like when they say your name?

Emotionally, what helps you feel in tune with your partner's feelings? What helps you feel connected during sex? Do you prefer extended foreplay or no foreplay? Does your desire for sex ebb and flow depending on how much effort your partner makes to have one-on-one time during the week?

Review what you've written about what you like most about touch, sensuality, and sex, and identify at least three things to share with your partner, though you can share more or everything. If you feel shy about describing to your partner what you like, especially physically, either point to your own body or draw a human body and circle specific areas. You may wait to have this conversation until you've also considered red-light behaviors and environment, or you can simply start the conversation with the green-light behaviors that work for you.

RED-LIGHT BEHAVIORS

Red-light behaviors are what doesn't feel good physically, verbally, and emotionally in regard to foreplay and sex.

Again, explore this first by writing in a journal, perhaps by using a chart like the one below. Starting with your head and working all the way down to your toes, what are the things that you don't particularly like, physically, verbally, and emotionally? Again, this isn't about identifying what a partner is doing wrong. It's simply about identifying our personal dislikes.

Sharing this with our partner is how we let them know what doesn't work for us.

Red-Light Behaviors		
Physical	*Verbal*	*Emotional*
I do not like my ears being touched.	*I do not like when my partner uses "dirty talk."*	*I do not like when my partner yells at me about something; it's hard for me to be intimate that night.*
I do not like when my partner pushes my head during oral sex.	*I do not like when my partner tells me to tell them specifics about their genitals during intercourse.*	*I do not like when my partner jokes and calls me the "old ball and chain" to his friends. It makes me feel unappreciated.*

Physically, what do you never want to do, or is there something you want to do less of? Do you not like being kissed in certain places? Do you not enjoy certain types of touch?

Verbally, are there things you don't want your partner to say? Are there particular phrases that turn you off?

Emotionally, are there behaviors that make you feel less inclined to have sex? Are there things your partner does that make you feel less connected?

Review what you've written and decide what you want to

share with your partner. You may wait until you complete the next section on environment so you can share all your thoughts at once or share this part now. Again, if you feel shy about describing or verbally telling your partner what you like, point to your own body or draw a human body and circle specific areas. The important thing is to communicate gently with your partner about what doesn't work for you.

Environment

Another important thing to consider is the context and physical environment for sexual experiences. Environment is a big factor that impacts how comfortable and safe we feel to be sexual. This isn't that different from setting the stage for any theatrical or musical performance. A lot of planning goes into making sure the audience is comfortable and in the right mood for the show.

When it comes to sex, consider these eight things, which are similar to creating the best environment for a concert: timing, venue, creativity, lighting, sound, temperature, privacy, and afterward.

As with green-light/red-light behaviors, I suggest writing about your preferences in a journal first, and afterward discussing them with your partner, so you both are already clear about each topic. If you and your partner differ on what you like, commit to at least trying one partner's preference one time and the other partner's preference another time.

1. **Timing:** Are you more spontaneous when it comes to sex or do you prefer to plan? If either of you is a planner, would it work to pick a certain time each week for sex, such as on date night? It may not seem romantic to plan sex, but that way, you both are making a commitment to connect sexually.

If you're more spontaneous, what sort of spontaneity do you prefer? Different places, times, and activities? Are you looking for your partner to initiate sex more to make it more exciting?

When it comes to sex, it's OK to want both spontaneity and planning. The goal of this conversation is to share what both partners prefer and do what feels most comfortable for both.

2. **Venue:** Is there a spot where you feel the most comfortable, like the bedroom? Or do you like sex in different places for excitement? Do you want to try something more risqué?

3. **Creativity:** Do you like your current sex life or do you want more variety? Do you want to add in costumes, toys, or products?

4. **Lighting:** Do you want the lights on or off? Would you like to see more of your partner, or are you self-conscious about your body and want low or no lighting? When partners have opposite preferences, a blindfold can be a good option, even just for more exhilaration.

5. **Sound:** Do you prefer quiet, to stay present, or does music help put you more in the mood? What type of music helps both of you feel sexy?

6. **Temperature:** Do you like the temperature colder or warmer? If you and your partner disagree on this, can you make a compromise on temperature?

7. **Privacy:** This is usually only an issue for partners with children, family members, or roommates living in the same house. Does it bother either partner to be sexual when other people are home? If so, can times be arranged when the house is empty? Are pets an issue,

and if so, can they safely be put in another room? If privacy at home is difficult or nonexistent, can you find other places for sex, like in your car?

8. **Afterward:** After sex, do you like to cuddle and talk, or do you like to immediately shower? If you and your partner have different preferences, can you compromise? After a shower, perhaps you can return to cuddling.

After you've considered your environment preferences on your own, you're ready for a sit-down conversation with your partner. If you haven't already discussed your green-light and red-light behaviors, you can include them in the same conversation. Choose who wants to go first, or you can flip a coin. Remember, the goal is to help each other learn what works for both of you. Ask questions to clarify what works or doesn't work.

It may feel strange or self-conscious to establish green-light/red-light behaviors and discuss the environment for sex, but we want the experience to be the most enjoyable. If we can create a better emotional and physical environment for sex, we can help foster intimacy. And you might learn something about your partner you didn't know!

Restoring sensuality and sexuality and creating a more satisfying sex life may take some time. However, by looking at resentments, exploring sensate focus therapy, and setting the scene, partners can rekindle romance and desire.

ISSUE 5

"I Don't Feel in Love with My Partner Anymore"

Remember when you and your partner first got together and felt inseparable? You couldn't wait until the next time you saw each other and that was all you thought about? What you felt was the intense rush of being in love.

Your partner may have been amazing, but hormones had more to do with this feeling. When we are in love, our brains produce three particular chemicals that foster these emotions. Noradrenaline stimulates adrenaline production and causes racing hearts and sweaty palms. Dopamine, also called "the feel-good chemical," stimulates pleasurable feelings. Finally, phenylethylamine gives us that butterfly feeling in our stomachs. All of these chemicals are released when we are in love.

Over time, these chemicals fade. This is not necessarily a bad thing. Imagine if those chemicals remained at the same high level forever? We would never want to leave our partners or do anything else.

Also over time, as the intensity of "being in love" fades, people may question their feelings for their partner. That's normal. After experiencing such an intense initial rush, our expectations get skewed. People can wonder if they still love their partner if "being in love" doesn't feel like it used to. There isn't the same rush, intensity, or excitement.

People who wonder where the feelings of being in love have gone need to recognize that those feelings aren't meant to last. It's hormonally impossible to sustain them. That doesn't mean people don't love their partner, but the experience of love, and even the nature of their love, changes. The first step to reconnecting, then, is to stay curious about and explore the nature of your love. Perhaps feelings of lust have been replaced by intimacy. True intimacy means loving someone in a more complete way on many levels; the sources of connection are deeper and more profound than simply romantic sexual attraction. The beautiful thing about true intimacy is that it can't be formed quickly. It takes time to grow, and it gains intensity over time. In other words, it's not something people experience right away, and not every couple can achieve it.

Here are three strategies to help partners "fall back in love" — and get those butterfly feelings again — as well as cultivate true intimacy. They are appreciating the continuum of long-term relationships, writing love letters, and understanding your connection style.

The Continuum of Long-Term Relationships

Sometimes we need to zoom out in order to zoom in. What does that mean? Sometimes we get so fixated on the now that we can't see the bigger picture. This strategy is about zooming out and stepping back to see the big picture of a long-term relationship.

Let's assume you're in a long-term relationship and you met your significant other in your twenties. Again, assuming all goes well in your relationship (you put in the work, time, and commitment), you'll be together into your seventies, eighties, or longer. Of course, during that time, over the course of fifty or sixty years, the road will not always be smooth. There will be bumps, blips, and challenges. Like any other healthy couple, you will have arguments or periods when things aren't always easy. But you commit to each other, work on the issues, and stay together until one of you passes on.

Imagine a graph that illustrates the ups and downs of this relationship over time. As the line moves horizontally, it would be jagged, almost like a heartbeat, with good times followed by challenging times followed by better times in an ongoing cycle. Zoom out, though, and the jagged line would look much smoother; only the biggest ups and downs would be noticeable. The line would look stable and overall probably ascending, since in this scenario, you, as a couple, are successfully meeting your relationship challenges.

When looking at the timeline over fifty years, do the individual zigzags matter? Not really, and not more than the overall growth. That's this strategy in a nutshell: To avoid focusing on and getting upset by downturns, focus on the overall long-term continuum.

Author Jonathan Haidt made a similar point in his book *The Happiness Hypothesis.* Haidt researched two kinds of love: passionate and companionate. Passionate love is romantic love; it's "being in love," when our hormones surge. Passionate love feels urgent and fills us with overwhelming happiness, euphoria, fear, and anxiety. It can feel like being on drugs. Haidt calls it "the love that you fall into."

Companionate love is more of a slow-burning fire. Haidt says companionate love "grows slowly over the years as lovers apply their attachment and caregiving systems to each other, and as they begin to rely upon, care for, and trust each other." In other words, passionate love is destined to burn out, while companionate love is destined to grow.

Haidt shows the difference in two graphs that track both types of love: one graph is of a six-month relationship, and one is of a sixty-year relationship. In the beginning, passionate love is way more intense than companionate love, which barely registers. Then, over the first six months, passionate love experiences steep peaks and valleys until both types of love are experienced as roughly equivalent in intensity. Now consider the sixty-year graph. Passionate love remains at a low intensity, and has much smaller peaks and valleys, while companionate love keeps getting stronger and stronger.

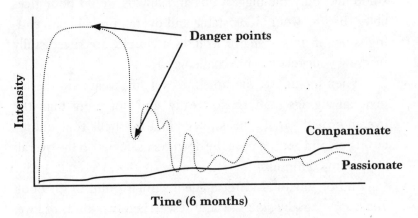

The Time Course of the Two Kinds of Love — Short Run

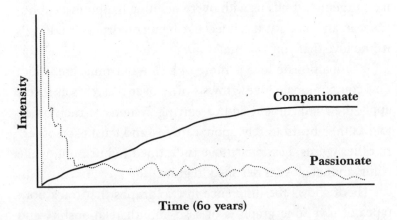

The Time Course of the Two Kinds of Love — Long Run

My imaginary graph of a long-term couple as well as Haidt's graphs are helpful ways to view a relationship. Even if someone is in a downturn, that doesn't mean the relationship will stay there forever, and seen from a long-term perspective, that dip in intensity will be just another blip. The trick is not to fixate on the blips. And if a couple has gotten through hardships before, that is even further confirmation that they can get through a blip again. Simply commit to your partnership for the long haul — blips, bumps, and all.

Love Letters

Think of a happy memory and picture yourself in that moment. Let's say it's a memory of being at the beach as a child. Recall that experience in all its sensory detail: like the seagulls chirping, and the grainy feeling of sand between your toes and the sand's texture on your skin. Remember the feeling of the cold ocean water splashing on your body and giving you goose bumps. Smell and taste the salt water as if it were yesterday. Imagine running around the beach with a childhood friend, laughing and smiling and falling into the wet sand. Whatever the memory is for you, bring it to life in your mind so you feel the happiness and joy again.

When partners don't feel the same love and sense of connection anymore, one way to rekindle it is to remember happy moments from the relationship. Those might feel distant, but they existed once, and like any happy memory, we can pull them up and put ourselves back into those fond memories by re-creating the moments in our mind.

The strategy I suggest is for partners to write love letters to each other. The letter should describe how the couple initially met and why the person fell in love. The letter should start at the beginning and go into detail: where they met, how old they were, the first meeting spot, what each person was wearing, the music that was playing — any and all sights, sounds, smells, sensations, and tastes. Then describe falling in love: The letter should describe the outings when the person experienced the rush of attraction and what they admired about the other. Was there a favorite shared experience that felt really special? What feelings arose?

Once each person has written their letter, they should get together and read their letters to one another. It doesn't matter who goes first as long as both people participate.

If you aren't sure what to write about or how to approach this love letter, here is a detailed hypothetical example of what I'm suggesting:

Dear Skylar,

I remember it was lightly raining the day we met. We initially met on the app Bumble and I was hesitant even chatting with you online because I wasn't sure if you were even real. You looked like someone who would be in a Ralph Lauren Polo ad. We had some really great banter over text before deciding to meet in person. We met at the Starbucks on Ventura in Studio City. It was so crowded I didn't see you at first, but when I did, I felt instantly calm. Like a feeling of home. You were taller than I expected but your smile really got my attention. It was genuine and real. I remember you were wearing a gray hoodie, still one of my favorites. I wore my favorite jeans and a tight blue zip-down top. I overthought that outfit at least five times before I left the house!

We sat at a table outside because by that time the rain had died down. I asked for a chai latte and you got some fancy sugary drink. I remember our conversation felt authentic. I liked how upfront you were. You asked the right questions, like you wanted to bypass the superficial crap that first dates usually go through. Afterward, we just couldn't stop texting. I loved that. My heart got jittery every time I heard the "ding" and a message came up from you. You made me laugh. A lot.

After that, we saw each other about once a week. I got nervous each date. My favorite date was when you took me horseback riding in Burbank. I almost fell off and you were so comforting. It was an adventure, but I felt safe with you. I also loved our Netflix nights where we would order Thai food and cuddle. I'd order the Thai papaya salad, but you'd always give me some of your pad thai.

Skylar, what I love about you is your ability to make me feel like I'm the only person in the room. You give me all your attention. I love how funny you are and how, even when I want to be mad at you, you have a way of making any situation lighter. Your intelligence challenges me. I really admire that you work hard for what you want, and it inspires me to do the same. I remember being so proud of you when you got your new job because you really deserved it.

I really appreciate the little things you did and still do for me. I loved that you would put my towel in the dryer to keep it warm for me after I'd shower. I remember one day when I had bad cramps, you gave me a hot water bottle for my tummy. Or even when you put your hand on my knee when we are driving. Those things mean a lot to me.

I know we are experiencing some challenges right now. But I also know us and our ability to get through hard times. Thank you for letting me go down memory lane with you — it reminds me of how special our relationship is. I love you.

Love,

Mia

It's amazing how we can shift our perceptions of a partner by remembering how we fell in love. It helps us focus on our connection and not as much on the issues. We remember the source of our bond. Sharing love letters is more than a reminder for the love partners once had; it's a way for them to remember the love that still exists.

Understanding Your Connection Style

When couples come to session and one partner explains that they don't feel loved by the other person, that person usually becomes immediately defensive. They might say, "What do you mean? I always want to have sex, and I am constantly giving you gifts." Then the partner looks defeated and responds by saying, "But you never tell me you love me!"

What is the disconnect here?

The way one person shows love may be different than how a partner *feels* loved. We need to understand our partner's connection style. When we show our partner love, it has to be conveyed in the ways they need.

One of the best tools I use in working with couples is helping them to understand their love language. Love languages are the way we give and receive love. The philosophy is based on Gary Chapman's book *The 5 Love Languages: The Secret to Love That Lasts.*

As the example shows, the way we show or give love may not be the best way for our partner to receive it. In this case, one partner is showing love in two different ways (physical touch and giving gifts), but the partner wants love to be verbally expressed (words of affirmation). If partners understand their love languages, they can better understand the best ways to express their love to their partner so they hear and receive it. The five love languages are acts of service, receiving gifts, quality time, words of affirmation, and physical touch.

Ideally, partners should read the following descriptions together and figure out their individual love languages. However, even if partners don't work on this together, understanding love languages can provide insight into why one or both partners don't feel loved by the other, as well as how to fix it.

Acts of Service

The love language "acts of service" means someone feels the most loved when their partner does things for them, like folding the laundry, running errands, or putting gas in the car. Typically, people whose love language is acts of service like to perform acts of service for people aside from their partner, too.

In order to express love to someone whose love language is acts of service, do the following:

- Help wash the dishes.
- Make a partner breakfast in the morning.
- Organize items in the house.

Receiving Gifts

The love language "receiving gifts" means people feel the most loved when they get a gift from their partner. Gifts don't have to be lavish or fancy; literally, it's the thought that counts. Those whose love language is receiving gifts usually remember exactly what gift they received and from whom because it means so much to them. They also give gifts as an expression of their love.

In order to express love to a partner whose love language is receiving gifts, try the following:

- Give flowers.
- Make a handwritten card.
- Buy ten small, inexpensive gifts, wrap them, and sprinkle them throughout the house.

Quality Time

The love language "quality time" means people feel the most loved when their partner spends uninterrupted time with them. This is about having someone's undivided attention, so they make eye contact, are active listeners, and don't check their phone or answer work calls when together. People with this love language also express love by providing quality time to their partner.

In order to express love to a partner whose love language is quality time, here are some ideas:

- Together take a long walk or hike.
- Cook together.
- As a couple go on a romantic trip.

Words of Affirmation

The love language "words of affirmation" means people feel the most loved when a partner tells them nice or uplifting things, like "I really appreciate you," and "Thank you for being a wonderful partner." They feel the most connected when their partner compliments or notices something they have done, and they often express love by voicing their feelings and appreciation.

In order to express love to a partner whose love language is words of affirmation, do the following:

- Tell the partner what is inspirational about them.
- Handwrite a note expressing gratitude and appreciation.
- Text the partner endearments and loving thoughts about the relationship.

Physical Touch

The love language "physical touch" means people feel the most loved when their partner hugs, massages, or holds their hand. While sex can be part of physical touch, people typically feel loved through any expression of touch. They also like to express their love in physical ways.

In order to express love to a partner whose love language is physical touch, try these ideas:

- Kiss the partner in public.
- Dance with the partner.
- Take a bath together.

Understanding your and your partner's love languages is a great way to deepen your connection. If you want to help discover your love language, take the comprehensive, thirty-question quiz on the 5 Love Languages website (see the notes).

Partners who need to rebuild their feelings of love for each other can do so by trying all these strategies: considering the continuum of long-term relationships, writing love letters, and understanding their connection style or love languages.

ISSUE 6

"I Do So Many More Chores!"

Chores. It's one of the most common arguments among couples. Who does what, who does more, whose turn it is — the list goes on. Let's simplify chores once and for all. If partners use a chore chart, appreciate each other, and become teammates, they will have a better distribution of chores and overall more respect for their partner.

Chore Chart

To work best, any system needs to be structured. Creating a structure can take time and work, but the payoff is organization and efficiency. Most couples don't talk about chores before they get into a relationship, so chores can often end up as a source of tension if one person gets frustrated because they are doing the majority of the load. However, when couples implement a structure for chores, this source of disagreement, resentment, and frustration gets resolved.

Before creating a chore chart, partners need to talk about their reasoning for wanting a chore chart. It's important to have this conversation when both partners are calm and emotions aren't high. In other words, don't talk about chore charts while standing over a pile of dirty laundry on the floor. Partners need to avoid blame and defensiveness and focus on resolving the issue by implementing a chore system. A sample request might be:

I want a chore chart because I'm hoping we can establish more equal responsibilities.

Or:

I want a chore chart so we don't forget who agreed to do which chores each week.

If partners have trouble talking, see the advice in Issue 1: "My Partner Doesn't Listen to Me" (page 5).

Then, once partners are clear on what chores or issues need to be addressed, create a chore chart. A chart is helpful because it ensures that household tasks are distributed evenly and everyone is aware of their responsibilities. When chores are defined and clearly displayed, neither partner can claim "I didn't know which chore I was supposed to do," or "I didn't realize that was my responsibility."

Here are six steps for creating a chore chart, followed by a sample chore chart that you can use as a template for creating your own. Or you can download a blank chore chart from my website, KelliMillerTherapy.com.

1. **Make a list of all the household tasks that need to be done.** This can include things like doing the laundry, cleaning the bathroom, walking the dog, washing dishes, vacuuming, paying bills, grocery shopping, and more.

2. **Assign tasks to each partner.** Consider each partner's strengths, preferences, and schedules when delegating tasks. For example, if one partner has to be at work early, they may not be able to walk the dog in the morning. Or if a partner has a degree in finance, they may want to take over the bills.

3. **Rotate other tasks.** Switch up chores both partners can do or struggle with (such as cleaning the toilets)

so the system feels equal. Choose a rotation schedule. For example, every week or month, partners can switch tasks.

4. **Determine a schedule.** Decide which day each task needs to be done and how often. For example, washing the dishes and walking the dog may need to be done every day, while vacuuming may only need to be done once a week.

5. **Display the chore chart in a visible place.** This way there is no question about who is doing what task and on what day.

6. **Schedule regular check-ins** to make sure that the chart is working effectively. Be open to making adjustments, and be flexible if you need to change tasks.

Chore Chart			
Day of Week	*Weekly Task*	*Week 1*	*Week 2*
Monday	Clean pet litter	Partner 1	Partner 2
Tuesday	Water plants	Partner 2	Partner 1
Wednesday	Mop floors	Partner 1	Partner 2
Thursday	Clean bathrooms	Partner 2	Partner 1
Friday	Do laundry	Partner 1	Partner 2
Saturday	Cut the grass	Partner 2	Partner 1
Sunday	Pay bills	Partner 1	Partner 2

A chore chart is a great tool to help divide household tasks. It's important for partners to communicate openly about what works for each of them but at the same time to be flexible in rotating tasks.

Appreciating Your Partner

It's not uncommon that we forget or take for granted the nice things our partners do for us. Things like taking out the trash or arranging dinner. After a while, these things may even shift from nice-to-haves to must-haves. We expect them. After all, shouldn't our partners be doing these things for us, anyway? Or if we do the majority of the chores, we may think our partner should *at least* take out the trash.

This entitled mentality is damaging to relationships. It assumes, since one person is doing nice things, the other is required to do the same. This may feel valid, but it also sets up an expectation that undermines appreciation and that the other person may not be aware of. If one person expects the other to do certain things, and the partner doesn't fulfill expectations, they have now disappointed the other. Then this can snowball into scorekeeping, where partners are mentally tallying who is doing more than the other. All of this can lead to dangerous resentments over how partners are fulfilling their part of the bargain. When this happens, it's better to start fresh — to declare previous expectations null and void and to rip up any mental tally sheets.

The antidote to entitled thinking is appreciation. Rather than focus on what a partner is not doing, we focus on what they are doing. To start appreciating a partner, we can try four strategies: positive feedback, background of chores, differences in execution, and hiring help.

Positive Feedback

Positive feedback means noticing the good things a partner does and telling them. It can be little things, like making dinner and cleaning up, and bigger things, like doing all the day's chores when a partner must work late. Try this yourself: Write down a list of at least ten things that your partner does that you appreciate. Then read the list to your partner.

Positive feedback goes a long way. If we are consistently telling our partners what they aren't doing, they can feel inadequate, frustrated, or underappreciated. Instead, by focusing on what is working, we can help rebuild communication and trust. As partners practice appreciation for what the other is doing, they both get positive reinforcement. It's a win-win.

Background of Chores

Another useful exercise is for partners to discuss how household chores were divided in their own homes growing up. Often, we model our own household division of labor without realizing it. Even unconsciously, we may feel the way chores were done in our childhood household is the "best way" because it is the most familiar. But people grow up in different environments, and there are many ways of operating a household. When partners understand where they both came from in regard to chores, this is another form of appreciation. We can have a deeper understanding of why our partner feels a certain way.

For example, Bella and Nico, a couple in their twenties, had recently moved in together. They struggled with chore division. I asked the couple about the ways chores were performed in their households growing up.

Nico said his mom did the "majority" of the chores, and his dad once in a while "took out the trash." He explained that he grew up in a household where his dad worked and his mom took care of him and his three sisters. His sisters would help his mom with chores, but he and his dad were often excused. Nico said there were arguments in the house because Nico's dad felt exhausted from working and Nico's mom was tired of "doing everything."

Bella said she had a very different experience. Bella grew up with her mother and her mother's partner. She stated that they equally shared household responsibilities. Bella says it felt "balanced," and they didn't fight about who did what in the house. They fought about other things, but household chores weren't an issue.

Nico said he never thought about how the way he grew up could impact his current relationship. But this helped him understand why he had a more traditional, "men don't do chores" attitude. Understanding Nico's background, Bella felt more compassionate, since a fairer approach hadn't been modeled for him. The couple agreed they wanted a more balanced and equal approach to chores, like Bella's parents. Once Bella and Nico talked about their childhoods, it helped them decide what kind of partnership they wanted, and this made it easier to figure out how to divide chores.

Differences in Execution

Another thing to keep in mind is that people perform chores differently. Not everyone manages tasks in the same way. Rather than criticize a partner for how they accomplish a task, the other person can appreciate them for doing it. Partners can appreciate each other's effort, even if the outcome isn't exactly to one or the other's liking. However, if one person is truly unhappy with the way a task is performed, they can offer to switch tasks.

Hiring Help

Finally, if partners can't resolve an unequal balance in household tasks, and it's causing stress in the partnership, they can consider hiring outside help. Delegating tasks to an outside company is another form of appreciation. It's appreciating that partners have tried and are now turning to alternative solutions to lessen the strain on the relationship. Hiring a cleaning service, setting up a meal-delivery service, or even hiring a person to run errands may alleviate some of the pressure.

Becoming Teammates

A relationship is a unit, and when it comes to chores, it helps to think of each other as teammates. Each person is an equal partner in creating and cleaning their shared dwelling. Teams can't exist without the help of all team members. By adopting this mindset, partners commit to helping each other in the spirit of sportsmanship, especially since chores can be boring. Bringing some comradery and excitement to chores is another opportunity to inject fun into a relationship.

Here are some ways to make chores fun as teammates:

- **Work together for a set time.** Set a timer for thirty minutes and see how much you and your partner can accomplish together in that time. Timing can add an element of rivalry that can make chores feel less daunting.
- **Compete with each other.** Set a timer, but this time see who can complete their assigned chores the fastest or the most efficiently. Each task wins a point, and at the end, the person with the most points gets a reward: choosing dinner, a massage, a small gift, and so on.
- **Incorporate role-play.** Combining sexy role-play with

chores can add a whole new element of excitement. One partner can choose the costume for the other person's chore. For example, for dusting and vacuuming, one person might dress as a French maid; for yard work, the person might dress as a farmer.

- **Add sensory elements.** Incorporating scents, sounds, or sights to chores can make them more enticing. Some good ideas are putting on a strobe light, adding candles for ambiance or scents, or listening to dance music.
- **Try a competitive chore swap.** Switch chores that are typically the other partner's responsibility, and each person can try to do them differently or better. Switching chores is also a great way to gain a better understanding of the other's responsibilities.
- **Add an element of surprise.** Put all the household chores in a bowl and have each partner pick one for the day or all of their tasks for the week. Picking chores from a bowl can add a little wonder into chore division.
- **Set up a cleaning co-op.** Ask friends if they would be willing to help clean in exchange for helping them clean. Make chores a fun social event with music and food and have some laughs.

Chores can be daunting, but partners are in it together. Appreciating this can lessen the physical and emotional load. Create a chore chart, appreciate what partners do, and become better teammates by incorporating new ways to conquer chores. This makes chores easier and adds fun to the relationship.

ISSUE 7

"We Can't Trust Each Other after Infidelity"

Discovering a partner has been unfaithful is a highly emotional and complicated experience. If processed properly, however, it can also be one of the most clarifying experiences for a relationship. When a partner is unfaithful, it can create feelings of betrayal, anger, confusion, and more, but when this breach is carefully and genuinely mended, it can result in more honesty, openness, and intimacy. In other words, although infidelity is a difficult process to overcome, it is not necessarily the end of a relationship. It can sometimes be an opening to an even better one.

Lexi and Vincent were a married couple in their late thirties who came to me because, a week prior, Lexi had discovered that Vincent had an affair with a coworker she knew. Understandably, Lexi was devastated and questioned if she could continue their marriage. It took many months to work through the pain, to understand how to fix what wasn't working in their relationship, and to find forgiveness. But ultimately, not only did Lexi and Vincent decide to stay together, but their relationship became even closer. Because of the work they each put in, they learned to communicate more openly and honestly, they established more equality between them, and they experienced a more authentic relationship going forward. I want to offer hope that it is possible to continue a partnership, and even create a deeper connection, after infidelity, but it does require effort by both people.

Navigating a relationship after infidelity takes work, time, and patience. Further, both partners need to want to work on and repair the relationship. Here are three tools that can help strengthen a partnership after infidelity: starting the forgiveness process, grieving and renewing your commitment, and understanding the affair and setting boundaries.

Starting the Forgiveness Process

If partners want to heal from infidelity, both partners need to do work to mend the relationship. Although the work among partners may look remarkably different, it takes the same amount of effort and commitment. This section summarizes the "footwork" forgiveness entails for both the unfaithful partner and the betrayed partner.

For the unfaithful partner, this means ending the affair and asking for forgiveness, which includes taking accountability for their actions. For the betrayed partner, this means remaining open to forgiveness, being open to trusting again, and rebuilding their own self-esteem in light of the affair. With time and dedication, and if both partners do their parts, the relationship can start to heal.

Footwork for the Unfaithful Partner

END THE AFFAIR

If couples are not in an ethically nonmonogamous relationship, meaning they have not discussed including outside partners, the affair outside the relationship needs to end. This step is essential for rebuilding the relationship. Ending the affair means that the partner involved stops and avoids all contact with the person they had the affair with. This might involve life changes in order to ensure this, such as creating physical distance. For example, if the outside person in the affair goes to the same gym as the partner, the partner needs to go to another gym. If the affair happened at work, it might require a new job. Unless the outside relationship is terminated, repairing the current one can't begin.

ASK FOR FORGIVENESS AND TAKE ACCOUNTABILITY

The unfaithful partner must take accountability for their actions and ask for forgiveness from their partner. A sincere, heartfelt apology includes the following five steps:

1. **Take accountability:** The first step in creating trust is to take accountability for what happened. This is not a time to blame the faithful partner for any problematic behavior of theirs. Those issues may be valid, but what's important initially is that the unfaithful partner take responsibility for choosing to have the affair. Taking accountability shows the faithful partner that the person is willing to grow, learn, and change. Here is an example: "I recognize I was completely wrong to have the affair, and I take ownership of the damage to you and to our relationship."

2. **Express remorse:** If the unfaithful partner doesn't express remorse, it's hard to convince the other person that infidelity won't happen again. Remorse acknowledges the self-inflicted harm and hurt on the person who had the affair, which is important to acknowledge. This includes regret, repentance, and the wish

that the affair never occurred, since it has hurt the faithful partner and jeopardized the relationship, which is considered more important than the affair. Here is an example: "I am so sorry that I did this to you. My behavior was absolutely wrong and I deeply regret it."

3. **Acknowledge the harm:** The unfaithful partners needs to recognize how the affair has impacted their partner and the relationship in all ways. This harm might go beyond the couple. Here is an example: "I understand how much my infidelity has damaged your trust in me and our relationship. I see how much harm this has created in our family and friendships."

4. **Commit to change:** The unfaithful partner must commit to never having another infidelity, as well as making whatever changes are necessary to repair and improve the relationship. They must commit to change, even if it takes time for the faithful partner to trust that commitment. In other words, this acknowledges that going forward the relationship will be different. Here is an example: "I understand it will take time to trust me again, but I promise to be completely faithful from now on, and I commit to doing whatever I can to save this relationship."

5. **Request forgiveness:** Forgiveness can only be requested. It can't be demanded or expected. Eventually, some form of forgiveness will be needed to fully repair the relationship, but that usually takes time. Renewed trust has to be earned. Here is an example: "I understand it might take some time, but I hope one day you can forgive me for having an affair."

Footwork for the Faithful Partner

When a faithful partner discovers a betrayal, they understandably experience a wide range of intense emotions. They should give themselves permission to feel whatever feelings arise. Then, if they decide to continue the relationship, starting the forgiveness process means simply remaining open to forgiveness and trust while rebuilding their self-esteem.

REMAIN OPEN TO FORGIVENESS

Forgiveness is a process, not an event. That means it might take some time to forgive and ultimately trust an unfaithful partner again. This doesn't happen overnight. The key, however, is to remain open to the possibility of forgiveness in the future, even though the faithful partner may not be ready to forgive today. This also means putting aside the desire to strike back or seek revenge.

REMAIN OPEN TO TRUST

Trust is built with consistency. Thus, if an unfaithful partner remains consistent in their commitment to end the affair and change, that eventually rebuilds trust. Remaining open to trust involves recognizing and acknowledging the work the unfaithful partner is doing to try to rebuild the relationship.

REBUILD SELF-ESTEEM

The process of forgiveness includes the faithful partner healing their own self-esteem. When infidelity occurs, it's natural for the faithful partner to feel bad about themselves. They may feel unwanted and unattractive, as if the way they look, act, or behave led to the affair. Regardless of the specific reasons for the infidelity — which are always complicated and usually related to existing relationship problems — the faithful partner must regain their sense of self-worth. That means practicing physical, emotional, and spiritual self-care, such as eating well, getting proper sleep, and seeking outside support. It includes replacing any negative self-talk ("I'm so unattractive") with positive self-talk ("I am worth loving").

If both partners each work on their part of the forgiveness process, the necessary healing will begin naturally. This requires patience on the part of both partners, both with themselves and with each other. Yet if both partners are willing to work through the challenges and make a conscious decision to rebuild their relationship, there is hope to create an even more emotionally intimate relationship.

Grieving and Renewing Your Commitment

An infidelity causes deep grief within a relationship. In this case, this grief is over the loss or death of the relationship both partners knew. That relationship has been irrevocably changed. Once partners grieve, however, they can allow room for a rebirth. That rebirth is the "new" relationship they start to rebuild. So these are related steps: grieving what has been lost while renewing a commitment to rebuild.

Grieving

Like forgiveness, grieving is a process. Grief doesn't look a particular way, and everyone's timeline for healing is different. Betrayed partners essentially experience grief in regard to infidelity in three parts: grief about the "old" relationship, grief about their partner's loyalty, and grief about their previously imagined future.

A helpful concept for understanding grief is Elisabeth Kübler-Ross's five stages of grief, to which David Kessler added a sixth stage. The six stages are denial, anger, bargaining, depression, acceptance, and finding meaning. Moving through the six-stage grief process can help partners move forward and renew their commitment.

DENIAL

Denial is often the first stage of grief because the body and brain are likely in shock. A common defense mechanism, denial is a way to avoid reality in order to protect ourselves. Denial may look like, "There is no way my partner cheated on me. We had a loving relationship."

ANGER

Anger is common in grief because, typically, underneath anger is hurt. People are hurt that their loved one was unfaithful. They may find themselves angry not just at their partner but at everyone or everything. Anger also gives the illusion of control because it's a powerful emotion. Anger looks like, "I'm so mad at my partner, and I can't believe they would do this to me!"

BARGAINING

Bargaining is a way to take back control of the situation. When people are in pain and uncomfortable, they try everything in their power to change the situation back to the way it was before the infidelity occurred. They may question what they could have done differently to prevent infidelity. Bargaining may look like, "If only I spent more time with my partner or was more attractive, my partner wouldn't have cheated."

DEPRESSION

Depression is a profound sadness. Everyone feels blue or sad once in a while, but the sadness of grief may feel unbearable. Depression shows up in different ways, but the most common signs are changes in sleeping habits, suicidal thoughts or ideation, confusion or distraction, eating more or less, and/or not wanting to do activities that once brought joy. Depression may look like, "I don't know if I can handle this or want to live; I am just too sad."

If you are currently experiencing suicidal thoughts, please don't hesitate to reach out for help, such as by calling the national Suicide & Crisis Lifeline (call or text 988, www.988life line.org).

ACCEPTANCE

Acceptance is recognizing that the event occurred. It doesn't necessarily mean forgiveness or being OK with what happened. It just means the person is processing what has happened and figuring out next steps. Acceptance looks like, "I understand this happened and I cannot change the past."

FINDING MEANING

Typically, the grief process culminates in finding meaning in the experience. This is especially important for partners who are overcoming infidelity and rebuilding a relationship. This involves exploring why the infidelity occurred as an opportunity to deepen and better understand the relationship in order to repair it. Finding meaning may look like, "I recognize this was very difficult for our relationship, but it allowed us to be more honest in our partnership going forward."

The grief stages aren't linear; stages can arise in different orders, ebb and flow, and last longer or shorter. The important thing to remember is that there is no wrong or right way to grieve. The main goal is to consciously process our emotions.

Renewing Your Commitment

Once both partners have worked through the grieving process enough to focus on finding meaning, they can begin to renew their commitment to each other. Renewing your commitment means recognizing you're now in a new relationship. The couple is grieving the old relationship and pledging to start a new one. The new relationship is an opportunity to incorporate the lessons learned from understanding the relationship problems that preexisted the infidelity.

STEPS TO RENEW YOUR COMMITMENT

1. **Determine what the new relationship will look like:** Each person should write down a list of what they need in the new relationship and some thoughts for how to realize them. For instance, if one partner names transparency and honesty, would that involve more check-ins throughout the day and/or more communication about the relationship? Are there new things partners need that they didn't need before? Partners should read and review their lists together.

2. **Express this renewed commitment:** Whether simply stating the words to each other or creating a commitment ceremony, partners should express their promises to each other. Writing down and/or stating new "vows" is a nice way to embody the new commitments the partners are making to each other.

3. **Create new shared experiences:** Creating new shared

experiences can be a nice way to create memories and associations with the new relationship. A shared experience can be picking up a new hobby together, such as playing pickleball, dancing, taking cooking classes, or volunteering. The idea is to create something new that didn't exist in the previous relationship.

4. **Create new daily rituals:** Creating new daily rituals is a way to ensure partners are connecting consistently. Rituals could include having breakfast in the mornings or walking together in the evening after work. For more ideas see "Quick Partner Connections" (page 32).

5. **Schedule check-ins about the relationship:** Communication about the new relationship is pivotal. It's important for partners to continue talking about what they need and how they feel the relationship is going. Aim for weekly or biweekly check-ins.

6. **Focus on the present:** It may be challenging to let go of an infidelity, but part of renewing a commitment is focusing on the new, current relationship and moving forward. It's important to put the past behind as partners create stronger accountability in the new relationship.

Grieving a relationship after infidelity is not only natural but necessary. If partners can truly mourn their feelings, they can start the process of reconstructing a new relationship. Renewing our commitment is a beautiful way to respect and honor our new relationship going forward.

Understanding the Affair and Setting Boundaries

Why infidelity occurs can be complex and unique to each person's situation, so it's important for partners to have open discussions together to understand why the affair happened. This requires strong communication, honesty, and a willingness to work through difficult emotions. If couples can identify clear problems to address, they can identify new boundaries to set that work for them both, and reshaping the new relationship can begin.

Understanding the Affair

It's natural for the faithful partner to have questions about the affair. This may be difficult to discuss, but it's important to talk about why and in what context the affair occurred. These answers may be necessary for understanding not only why the infidelity happened in the first place but also for constructing the new relationship.

To begin, it's important that the unfaithful partner respect their partner's curiosity about why the affair occurred. Second, the unfaithful partner should be transparent with their answers, as difficult as that might be for both parties. It's also OK if the faithful partner doesn't want to ask any questions or know any answers — that is their choice. If at any point the conversation gets too heated, it's OK to utilize time-outs to get recentered. See "Time Outs" (page 19) for more information.

Here are some sample questions the faithful partner may want to ask, but this list is only a guide. Depending on the people and the circumstances, the faithful partner may want further clarification of some issues and no information about others.

QUESTIONS FROM THE FAITHFUL PARTNER

1. What do you want me to know about this affair?
2. What did the affair mean to you?

3. What parts of yourself did you rediscover? If so, do you think you can show me those new parts?

4. Looking back, were there needs you couldn't express to me — intellectually, emotionally, physically, or otherwise?

5. Did the affair have anything to do with our sex life? If so, would you want something different sexually going forward?

6. Did you see the affair as a sign that something was missing between us? If so, what exactly?

7. What do you believe are the strongest parts of our relationship?

8. What would have been the biggest loss if we decided not to work on this?

9. Why do you want to come back to the relationship?

10. What do you hope about our relationship going forward?

Setting Boundaries

Finally, to move forward, the couple needs to identify and set clear boundaries in their new relationship. Boundaries set limits and give clarity and structure within a relationship. They ensure both partners are clear on the guidelines of the relationship.

There are a variety of boundaries to consider, and what constitutes an "appropriate" boundary will vary among couples. Partners should sit down together and have an open dialogue about the boundaries of their new relationship. The most important takeaway is that boundaries are designed to help a couple figure out the safest and most comfortable ways to be together.

Below, I raise questions related to boundaries concerning

commitment, sexuality, emotions, time, privacy, and communication.

COMMITMENT

What defines commitment in the relationship? Is it remaining physically faithful? Emotionally faithful? What does remaining faithful look like specifically? Alternatively, what constitutes cheating in the relationship?

SEXUALITY

This can involve setting limits related to physical touch, personal space, and sexual intimacy. What defines a sexual relationship to both partners? Do both want a sexually monogamous relationship? Is either partner looking for an open or ethically nonmonogamous relationship? If so, what are the rules for that type of relationship?

EMOTIONAL

This involves setting boundaries around emotional expression, sharing personal information, and expectations of emotional support. Do both partners want an emotionally monogamous relationship? Is either looking for emotional or intimate connections with others? Is an emotional relationship OK with ex-partners from the past?

TIME

Partners can establish boundaries around how much time they spend together and apart. Do partners feel comfortable spending time with others outside the relationship if there is an attraction or past history? Are there limits on who a partner can and cannot spend time with? Alternatively, could a partner spend time with someone else if the other partner has knowledge or consent?

PRIVACY

How do partners feel about privacy? Are certain aspects of privacy OK? Or do partners feel it is necessary for both to give up their privacy, including access to their phone, email, and social media accounts?

COMMUNICATION

Setting boundaries around communication can include what is and is not acceptable in terms of tone, language, and subject matter. How do partners feel about communication in respect to social media and texting? Can a partner communicate with anyone online? Or are there limits on who a partner can and cannot communicate with without the other partner's knowledge or consent?

After infidelity, it is possible to repair and even rebuild the relationship. Speaking openly about the affair can help a couple understand what wasn't working in the relationship and shed light on what can help the relationship going forward. Beneficial tools for healing include starting the forgiveness process, grieving and renewing a commitment, and understanding the affair and setting boundaries.

"We Are Too Culturally Different"

People are all wired differently. That means we all think and process in unique ways. People may have similarities in the way they think, but ultimately we have our own individual thought processes. This is what makes the world so distinctive. We can learn from each other and gain various different perspectives because we are all coming at life from different angles.

I remember playing a game in elementary school. The teacher asked us to take out a piece of paper and colored pencils. She told us to draw what she was describing. For about ten minutes, she narrated a situation while we went to work visualizing it. After she was finished, she asked us to each show our drawings to everyone in the class. All thirty pictures looked completely different. How is that possible? She described the same scene to all of us, but we each perceived what she was describing differently.

All of which is to say, no two people see and think the same way, which is a result of different upbringings, cultures, races, religions, and more. In fact, partners can share the same race, religion, or ethnicity and still experience cultural differences, perhaps because they grew up in different cities. In other words, partners can feel culturally different for many reasons.

Studies show that there are more multicultural relationships today than in previous generations. That means we need an even greater understanding of various cultures or lifestyles.

With our partners, understanding their culture and upbringing can prevent misinterpretations and create harmony. The three strategies I recommend for doing this are learning about each other's cultures, incorporating traditions from each other's cultures, and having fun experiencing each other's cultures.

Learning about Culture

The best way to prevent misunderstandings is through education. In this case, learning about our partner's culture and sharing our own. Culture represents shared beliefs, values, customs, behaviors, and practices, and these can be related to ethnicity, race, religion, lifestyle, geography, and more. People often develop misconceptions about other cultures, and partners can have misconceptions they aren't even aware of. Even if partners share a common culture, learning how they each experience it can still be beneficial.

In essence, this strategy is simply about partners asking each other a series of questions about their cultures. If you don't know the answers, that's OK, but it might be interesting to take this opportunity to learn more about your own heritage, such as by asking relatives or taking a DNA test to find out your ancestry.

People take pride in where they come from, and they usually like it when people take interest in their background, especially their partner. I suggest approaching this conversation in a spirit of openness to learn things we never realized or had a chance to share before.

Partners should take turns answering these questions on the following topics:

Traditions: What are your family traditions? Can
   you describe your favorite tradition or the most

authentic? Are there lesser-known cultural traditions or ones you want to learn more about?

Language: What language did your family speak in the house? Did your relatives all share that language? If that family language is unfamiliar to the partner, write something in that language so they can see how it looks.

Art: What is your country's art like? Can you describe the style or share some visuals? Is there a particular artist or artwork that you feel best represents your country?

Music: What music did you grow up listening to? Can you play some of your favorite music and describe why you like it? Partners should compare the different types of music that defined their upbringings.

Food: What are some typical foods that your family ate? What is your favorite meal? What tastes and flavors define your culture's cuisine?

Social norms: What were the social norms in your family and culture growing up? Do they differ today and from your partner? What are some mistaken assumptions people make about your culture's social norms?

Geography: Where you are from? On a map, show this exactly. What neighboring cities or countries had an impact on the region where you lived? Was there conflict or peace among peoples, cultures, and nations?

History: What is the history of your family and of the country where you grew up? What hardships did your family face? Who is your favorite historical figure from your country and why?

Economics: What was the economic status of your family growing up? Did it differ from the economic status of your region or country? If partners are from different countries originally, perhaps share examples of their currency.

Politics: What were local or national politics like for you growing up? Do you have any political opinions on the current situation in the country you're from?

Religion: Did your family observe a particular religion? Do you or they still practice? What other religions were practiced where you grew up? Describe any important rituals people practiced.

People: Describe the community you grew up in. What were people like — more reserved or more open? What characteristics define the people where you are from? What do you feel is important to know about them?

We all come into this world with preconceived notions. It's helpful to get educated about cultures and specifically our partner's. This knowledge will help us understand how our partners operate in certain situations and why.

Incorporating Traditions

At times, partners can feel disconnected because of their different backgrounds. Their cultures may feel unfamiliar because they don't have any experience with them. This can lead to frustrations when one person does things that feel completely out of alignment with the way the other person does things.

Ira and Kate were a couple in their thirties. Ira was Jewish and lived in a town outside of New York City. Kate was born in the United States, but her parents were born in Ireland. Kate talked about the discomfort she felt when she went to Ira's family for dinner. She felt the family was "loud," and she couldn't get over how everyone talked about their issues so openly. She felt uncomfortable at times. Ira said the opposite. *He* felt uncomfortable going to Kate's parents' home because no one really talked and it felt "awkward" sitting at the table.

Kate and Ira were unfamiliar with each other's cultures. I validated these feelings but then asked a question that surprised them both. I asked them to name their favorite thing about their partner's culture. Kate said she loved how education was valued in Jewish culture. Laughing, she added, "And I really love matzo ball soup!" Ira said he loved the Irish music Kate's parents played and Irish soda bread, which he'd never had before. I then asked the couple to incorporate both traditions into their own household. For Kate, that involved having educational readings on Tuesdays and making matzo ball soup from scratch based on Ira's mom's recipe. For Ira, that involved playing (and dancing to) Irish music with Kate on certain date nights and finding the most authentic soda bread he could find as a special dessert afterward.

What are your favorite traditions or values from your partner's culture? How can you incorporate them into your home and partnership?

For example, if one partner is Chinese and celebrates the Chinese New Year, the couple could consider giving each other red good-luck envelopes containing personal notes of good wishes instead of money. Adapt this same approach to any applicable cultural tradition, honoring it while also making it your own.

Incorporating traditions from partners is important because it unifies them as a couple. The focus is no longer on differences that cause conflicts but embracing differences we enjoy and making new traditions together.

Having Fun Experiencing a Partner's Culture

Another way to approach cultural differences in a relationship is to have fun experiencing each other's culture. We can often focus on what is not working, and a partner's culture is intrinsic to who they are; it's something they can't and won't change. So work to bridge any culture gap. The goal here is not only to learn about a partner's upbringing, values, and culture but to share and participate in them. Incorporating these activities can bring two people closer together.

Here are some ideas for having fun culturally:

- **Quiz each other on your culture:** Look up facts about your culture and see how well your partner does in answering them. The person who wins could get a small prize, massage, or dinner choice.
- **Cook cultural meals together:** This works even if you're from the same country. Use your favorite recipe from your family or find a brand-new recipe and make it together. Alternatively, surprise each other with food from your partner's family of origin.
- **Learn your partner's language:** Obviously, if partners have the same language of origin, this doesn't apply, but if not, why not learn a little of your partner's language? Even if it's just a few words, it's fun to be able to speak to your partner in their family tongue. Alternatively, partners could learn a family language together, one neither knows.

- **Travel to a partner's home country or city:** A great way to experience a partner's culture is to visit that culture together.
- **Play games from a partner's culture:** Get competitive by playing board games, card games, or sports from a partner's culture.
- **Attend a cultural exhibit:** Seek out exhibits related to a partner's culture and attend together.
- **Volunteer in a partner's community:** Volunteering is a wonderful opportunity to not only serve a community but to meet people from it and get to know them.
- **Watch cultural TV shows:** View TV shows or movies from a partner's culture and discuss the themes, language, and social norms.
- **Visit cultural landmarks:** Attending museums, religious sites, and art galleries associated with a partner's culture can be a great activity.
- **Wear cultural clothing:** Experience traditional clothing from a partner's culture. Take photos together to capture the experience.
- **Follow cultural influencers:** Discuss how an influencer from a partner's culture represents their country in a positive or negative way. Use influencers to learn about new trends, perspectives, and cultural news.

When we focus on differences, we can forget about having fun. But having fun in ways related to our partner's culture can help us learn about our partner and enable us to step out of our comfort zone and have more engaging experiences.

Although it can be challenging when partners are from different cultures, this can also be an opportunity for enrichment. It can enhance personal growth, promote a deeper appreciation of the world, and foster empathy for differences. Try all these approaches: learning about a partner's culture, incorporating traditions, and having fun in culturally related ways.

ISSUE 9

"We Spend Money Differently"

Money is one of the top complexities in a relationship. This is because money is closely tied to our emotions. Our need for financial stability affects our identity, self-worth, and well-being. Too much or too little income can create power dynamics in a relationship, spark a fear of judgment from partners, and influence personal values. Given the gravity of the impact of money, it's no wonder so many couples struggle with it.

Despite the challenges, it's important to talk openly about money in a relationship. Honest conversations around money can help build trust and understanding and help couples work toward shared financial goals.

Here are three strategies for getting comfortable talking about money and being fully transparent about finances: setting financial goals, generating a budget, and creating an emotional inventory around money.

Setting Financial Goals

Piper and Jake were a couple in their forties. They felt they were "soul mates" but could not see eye to eye on money. They felt they had different spending habits that impacted their plans for the future. It often caused daily arguments, and they didn't know how to resolve their differences.

When I sat down with the couple, one of the first things we

talked about was each of their individual short- and long-term financial goals. Surprisingly, they both looked stunned. They had been so caught up in their day-to-day arguments with money that neither had taken the time to think about their goals.

As a starting point, I told Piper and Jake we'd use a process I created called CLOSER, which stands for communicate honestly, list goals, organize priorities, set specific goals, envision a plan, and review goals.

Communicate honestly: Talk about your financial situation. Discuss openly any debt, expenses, and income you both have.

List goals: What do you want to achieve financially as a couple, both short-term and long-term? Short-term goals are usually achievements within the next one to three years. These could include things like paying off credit card debt or setting up an emergency fund. Long-term goals might be saving for a down payment on a home or starting a child's education fund.

Organize priorities: Which goals are most important to you as a couple, and which ones do you want to focus on first? It might be helpful to separate the goals into "must-haves" like paying off credit card debt and "fun-to-haves" like planning a tropical vacation. Organization could also involve delegating expenses to each partner. For example, one partner will pay for utilities while another pays for rent.

Set specific goals: Once you have identified your shared financial goals, make them specific and quantifiable. For example, instead of saying, "I'm going to pay off my credit card debt," set a specific goal, like: "I'm going to pay a hundred dollars each month to lower my credit card debt."

Envision a plan: Once you have set your short-term and long-term financial goals, create a plan to achieve them. If you haven't done so already, create a budget (see "Generating a Budget," below), set up automatic savings or debt repayment, and/or look into other ways to increase your income.

Review goals: Periodically review your goals. Life circumstances change, so it's important to be flexible and adaptable.

CLOSER worked well for Piper and Jake. Piper wanted to save to buy a place together, and Jake was set on having yearly vacations. So we figured out their short- and long-term goals and distinguished their must-haves and fun-to-haves. This good organizational exercise allowed for both of their interests. Piper was surprised Jake also wanted some of the things she wanted. And Jake realized that thinking about finances broadly helped him envision what they needed to work toward.

Outlining your financial goals, whether for yourself or for your partnership, helps to create a better understanding of what you want to achieve financially. Utilizing CLOSER can unify you as a couple, remind you of your joint financial intentions, and create a concrete path for how to get there.

Generating a Budget

Top financial advisers suggest creating a budget, whether we are single or in a partnership. Creating a budget helps us feel more in control of our finances. It also assists us in understanding our spending habits, saving money, planning for the future, and reducing financial stress.

If you are sharing finances, create the budget together. If you keep your finances separate, each person can create their own individual budget, but share your budgets to help with joint accountability with spending.

The thought of creating a budget often scares people. It may feel overwhelming, constricting, or even boring. But creating a budget will actually give you freedom; recognizing this can help alleviate some fears. Understanding and planning your financial situation will enable you to spend more wisely. If you know what you're able to spend, you'll be less worried about overspending and feel more in the driver's seat of your finances.

Follow these steps to start:

1. **Calculate your net income or your final profit:** Net income is your total income after taxes, interest payments, and business expenses. Make a list of all the sources of income you have in a month, including salary, bonuses, stocks, and any other related sources minus taxes and expenses.

2. **Generate a list of expenses:** List all your monthly expenses, including things such as rent/mortgage, utilities, groceries, health insurance, gym memberships, car payments, subscriptions (entertainment apps, newspapers, charity donations, etc.), and any other expenses.

3. **Categorize these expenses:** For example, rent would be "housing," the electric bill would be "utilities," and so on. See the chart below for ideas.

4. **Set a target budget for each category:** Decide on the amount of money you want to allocate to each category. Set realistic goals that are easily obtainable. For example, a target for groceries could be four hundred dollars a month. Another approach is to use the 50/30/20 rule: This rule suggests that 50 percent of income should go toward necessities (like rent, groceries, and so on), 30 percent toward optional spending (entertainment, travel, and so on), and 20 percent toward savings and/or debt repayment.

5. **Monitor your spending:** Keep a record of all your spending in each category throughout the month. Be gentle with yourself, as you are trying a new path of saving and spending.

6. **Review and adjust your budget:** At the end of each month, review your budget to see if changes are needed.

7. **Use a budgeting app:** If it feels difficult to track your budget on your own, consider using a budgeting app to track expenses and stay within budget.

Generating a budget is a great starting point for appreciating your spending habits. Your budget can always change, depending on your needs or finances, but being proactive can put you in control of your money. On the next pages is a chart with categories and budget items to get you started. You can download this chart on my website, KelliMillerTherapy.com.

Budget	
Expense	*Cost Per Month*
VEHICLE/TRANSPORTATION	
Gas or electric car charging fees	
Bus/subway fare	
Insurance	
Maintenance	
Repairs	
Registration fees	
Parking fees	
HOUSING	
Mortgage/rent	
HOA fees	
Repairs and maintenance	
Housecleaner / cleaning supplies	
Lawn/yard/garden	
Property taxes	
Homeowners/renters insurance	
Home warranty	
UTILITIES	
Water	
Electric	
Cable	
Internet	
Garbage	

FOOD	
Groceries	
Restaurants	
ENTERTAINMENT	
Activities	
Travel	
Media/streaming subscriptions	
MEDICAL	
Health insurance	
Dental insurance	
Specialty care	
Mental health	
Prescriptions	
PERSONAL	
Personal care / toiletries	
Cell phone	
Gym membership	
Haircuts	
Clothing/shoes	
Gifts	
Charitable donations	
MONEY	
Student loans	
Retirement account	
Life insurance	
Debt payments	

Budget (*continued*)	
Expense	*Cost Per Month*
CHILDREN	
Childcare	
Clothing/shoes	
School fees	
Sports / after-school activities	
Camps	
Entertainment for kids	
Books	
PETS	
Food/treats	
Grooming	
Veterinarian	
Pet insurance	

Creating an Emotional Inventory

When couples argue about finances and it creates conflict between them, it's important to do an emotional inventory on money. Essentially, this involves cataloging what money means to you and your partner by answering a list of questions. Understanding our emotions around money, the messages we receive as children about money, and our anxieties surrounding money can give us greater insight into why we're arguing.

Each person should create their own emotional inventory by answering each question below separately:

1. What does money represent to you?
2. What types of emotions does money bring up for you?
3. How was money handled in your family growing up?
4. How, if at all, was money talked about in your family growing up?
5. Did you feel like you had enough money, or were you worried about money as a child?
6. In your culture specifically, what are the messages surrounding money?
7. What are your biggest fears or anxieties surrounding money?
8. What do you believe are the societal messages surrounding money?
9. What kind of power dynamics do you believe money creates?
10. How do you feel about debt?
11. How do you feel about spending money on things you enjoy?
12. Do you ever feel guilty or indulgent when you spend money?
13. How do you feel about saving money?
14. Have you ever had a conflict with someone (besides your partner) about money? What happened and how was it resolved?

Once each person fills out their inventory, they share their answers openly with their partner. Ideally, the responses will give each partner insight and a deeper understanding of what money means to the other. Try not to make any judgments based on a partner's responses, but be open to understanding how their answers could influence their current financial situation.

For example, Tal and Harry, a couple in their fifties, came to my office because they couldn't stop arguing over money.

Tal was a saver while Harry was a spender. Tal couldn't understand why Harry couldn't stop spending, especially because they wanted to buy a house together. I had them each do an emotional inventory around money. Harry's answers gave a deeper understanding about what finances meant to him and how it affected his relationship with Tal. Below are Harry's answers.

1. What does money represent to you? *Money represents power, freedom, and entitlement.*

2. What types of emotions does money bring up for you? *It brings up fear (that I won't have enough), power, control, security, and value.*

3. How was money handled in your family growing up? *I could tell my parents struggled with financial issues. I heard my parents argue a lot about money and it scared me. My dad constantly told me and my siblings that money was the answer to all problems. He would have nice watches and suits and told us that was the key to being respected. My mom was constantly spending and had nice bags, clothes, and jewelry. She'd often sneak purchases without my dad knowing.*

4. How, if at all, was money talked about in your family growing up? *Money was only talked about in terms of possessions. I would overhear my mom saying to my dad that Mrs. Jones got a new ring, or my dad would talk about the new car that his boss bought. But we never talked about budgeting or saving.*

5. Did you feel like you had enough money, or were you worried about money as a child? *I was definitely worried about money as a child. I think it was confusing because of the nice things my parents had, but then*

there were complaints there wasn't enough money. I also knew how important money was to both of them.

6. In your culture specifically, what are the messages surrounding money? *Money is strength, respect, fulfillment, competency, success. If you don't have it, you're not valued or enough.*

7. What are your biggest fears or anxieties surrounding money? *That I won't have enough and that if I don't have enough, I won't be enough for my partner. That in order to be loved, I need to have nice things.*

8. What do you believe are the societal messages surrounding money? *That if you have money, you are successful. But also that there is no limit on too much money. More money equals more happiness.*

9. What kind of power dynamics do you believe money creates? *The person who has more is in control. The person who has less money is inferior.*

10. How do you feel about debt? *It terrifies me, but I avoid thinking about it. I worry my partner will find out how much debt I have.*

11. How do you feel about spending money on things you enjoy? *At times it feels OK. Other times I feel like I "shouldn't" because of the debt I have.*

12. Do you ever feel guilty or indulgent when you spend money? *Not immediately. But for sure later or when my partner finds out.*

13. How do you feel about saving money? *I think it's very important, but I struggle with actually doing it.*

14. Have you ever had a conflict with someone (besides your partner) about money? What happened and how was it resolved? *Yes, I had a friend borrow money, and he never returned it. I never said anything, and eventually our friendship dissolved.*

Harry's inventory provided a lot of insight. Given his childhood, it's clear where Harry got the messages about how money represented importance, value, and success. It also makes sense why Harry spends it because this provides a sense of power, importance, and control. With the insight from his inventory, Harry was able to understand more about why he was spending. He was also able to admit to Tal how he was scared he wasn't enough by not having as much money.

When partners explore their emotional inventories, they can gain a deeper recognition of their emotions surrounding money. Uncovering insights will help both partners have more empathy about money issues and be more effective in planning for the future.

Money can be an emotional topic, which is one of the reasons it creates such hardship among couples. We can have a better relationship and understanding about money by setting goals, generating a budget, and reflecting on our emotions by creating an emotional inventory.

ISSUE 10

"My Partner or I Have an Addiction"

A ddiction is the inability to stop using a substance or participating in a behavior even though it is causing psychological, emotional, and/or physical harm. Addictions are complicated and need treatment with a licensed professional because they have underlying emotional and psychological causes that need to be addressed. Most importantly, some addictions can be fatal and require immediate attention. If you or your partner are struggling with an addiction and have not yet sought help, please contact the Substance Abuse and Mental Health Services Administration (SAMHSA) National Helpline (800-662-4357; www.samhsa.gov/find-help/national-helpline). Please know there is no shame in getting help. Millions of people across the world do it every day, and they are thankful for it.

Recovery from addiction is possible, but it takes honesty, commitment, a strong support system, and lifestyle changes. Assuming partners have sought treatment or are currently undergoing treatment for an addiction, there are three tools that can help with the process: understanding addiction, planning for recovery, and identifying your negative voice.

Understanding Addiction

Addiction is a global phenomenon that affects millions of people worldwide regardless of their background, education, or socioeconomic status. Education about addiction is paramount.

Understanding addiction can help partners learn about the process, what it means to have an addiction, and how to plan for recovery. This includes understanding what an addiction is, signs of addiction, and the types of addictions people experience.

An addiction is the condition of being physically and/or psychologically dependent on a particular substance or behavior despite negative consequences. In simple terms, an addiction is when someone's life has become unmanageable because of dependency. Addiction is multifaceted and complex, and there are various physical and psychological components of the disease.

Typical signs of addiction include but are not limited to the following:

- A strong urge to use a substance or engage in a behavior which the person can't control.
- Physical or emotional withdrawal symptoms when the person tries to stop using the substance or engaging in the behavior. Physical symptoms could include sweating, nausea, vomiting, and so on, while emotional symptoms could include anxiety, depression, anger, and so on.
- Spending time thinking or obsessing about, obtaining, using, or recovering from the substance or behavior.
- Continuing to use the substance or engage in the behavior despite negative consequences. For example, this could include continuing to drink alcohol despite kidney issues, continuing to gamble despite being in debt, or continuing to overexercise despite multiple knee injuries.
- Developing a tolerance to the substance or behavior. Tolerance is when someone needs more of the substance or behavior to get the same effect. For example,

a person needs two or three glasses of wine to feel the same effects as when they once drank one glass.

Addictions come in various forms and manifest differently in every individual. The most common addictions include the following:

Substance addictions: addictions to drugs, alcohol, and prescription medications

Behavioral addictions: addictions to activities, such as shopping, gambling, pornography, sex, romantic love, video games, and social media

Work addictions: addictions to work or career, such as engaging in excessive working hours and neglecting personal relationships

Food addictions: addictions to certain types of foods, excessive amounts of food, a preoccupation with food, or food-restricting behaviors

Exercise addictions: addictions where there is an excess of exercise or physical activity to the point where it interferes with a person's daily life or causes physical harm

Addiction stems from a variety of factors, including environmental, cultural, social, personal, and genetic. Studies have identified multiple genes associated with addiction as well as genes associated with addiction to specific substances.

Recovery from addiction is challenging but possible with the right treatment, support, and resources.

Planning for Recovery

When one partner has an addiction, it's essential both partners seek recovery. Although it is of primary importance for the partner with addiction to seek help first, it's recommended that their partner seek help as well. Addiction affects all those involved, and it's important that both partners have adequate support during recovery.

There is no single specific approach to addiction recovery. The most effective plan of action depends on the partner's specific needs, circumstances, and type of addiction. The most important elements, however, are honesty, consistency, and commitment to the recovery process. Recovery help may look similar in certain areas for the addicted partner and the partner of the addict.

For the addicted partner:

1. **Obtain treatment:** It is vital for the addicted partner to seek treatment for their addiction. Treatment centers are geared toward specific addictions, so it is best to utilize the center that caters to the specific addiction. A primary physician or mental health therapist can help find the right treatment center. Additionally, there are online resources that can direct people to the right care.

2. **Seek a licensed therapist:** Recovery is difficult to do alone and requires consistent care. Sobriety is most effective when supported by weekly therapy. It is best to choose a therapist who understands and specializes in addiction and trauma, if needed. Therapy modalities vary based on the therapist but can include cognitive behavioral therapy, family therapy, mindfulness, and more. Trauma-focused modalities include eye movement desensitization and reprocessing (EMDR), brainspotting, somatic experiencing, and more.

3. **Attend group support meetings:** Support groups, specifically 12-step groups, are a wonderful way to

maintain sobriety. It's best to choose a group that focuses on the person's specific addiction. For example, Alcoholics Anonymous, Sex and Love Addicts Anonymous, Cocaine Anonymous, Overeaters Anonymous, and so on. Addiction groups provide a supportive community with like-minded individuals and peer-to-peer accountability. Alternative non-12-step support groups are also an option. These include SMART Recovery, Refuge Recovery, and LifeRing Secular Recovery.

4. **Identify feelings:** It's important for someone to understand what they're feeling without judgment in order to prevent a relapse. A great way to examine feelings and alternative ways to get through the feeling without using is the technique "Using the Mirror on Why" (page 155).

5. **Identify triggers and avoid them:** The person should write a list of triggers, which can include people, places, and things. Be specific and then avoid those triggers in order to support successful recovery. For example, if walking into the grocery store triggers someone when they see the alcohol aisle, they might consider having their groceries delivered instead. Or if someone struggles with gambling and their best friend loves to go to the casinos, they might limit contact with that friend for the time being to help avoid gambling. It's best to avoid people, places, and things that increase a chance of relapse.

6. **Consider medications:** When used in combination with therapy, some medications can be helpful in treating addiction. Medications can be used to manage withdrawal symptoms, reduce cravings, and block

the effects of drugs or addictive behaviors. Ask a medical doctor for more information.

7. **Utilize integrated approaches:** Certain practices can be helpful to manage stress and anxiety, which include exercise, yoga, meditation, and mindfulness practices. Apps such as Headspace, Calm, and Insight Timer can help guide someone who is a first timer with mindfulness. Anything that helps relieve stress can help someone avoid acting out.

For the partner of the addict:

1. **Seek a licensed therapist and/or a support group:** It is recommended that the partner of an addict get help as well. Therapy and support can help them manage the difficulties of living with an addicted partner. It is best to choose a therapist who understands and specializes in addiction. Support groups are wonderful places to meet individuals going through a similar experience. Al-Anon, Nar-Anon, Families Anonymous, SMART Recovery Family & Friends, and Co-Dependents Anonymous are all available to help partners of those struggling with an addiction.

2. **Practice self-care:** Often when someone focuses on their partner and their struggles, they forget about their own needs. It's important that both partners get proper rest, meals, and exercise, as well as find activities that bring joy. Recovery starts with having a fulfilling life outside of a partner's addiction.

3. **Support the addicted partner:** People should let the addicted partner know they will be supported through this long and difficult process. It might be helpful to ask specifically what an addicted partner needs to maintain sobriety.

4. **Avoid enabling behavior:** Enabling behavior means making a partner's addiction easier for them. Partners may not even be aware of how they can enable their addicted partner. Enabling behavior looks like making excuses for the partner, covering up for them, giving them money for their addiction, or trying to control their behavior.

5. **Communicate with the addicted partner:** It's OK to actively listen to an addicted partner and their struggles, but it's equally important for the other person to express their struggles. It's also pivotal to set boundaries with an addicted partner. For example, that disrespectful behavior or lying won't be tolerated.

6. **Remove any blame:** It's easy for a partner to assume they play a vital part in their partner's addiction. They should utilize the three Cs from the Al-Anon program: "I didn't _cause_ it, I can't _control_ it, and I can't _cure_ it." This is a helpful reminder that the partner's addiction and recovery journey is theirs and not the other person's fault.

Recovery from addiction takes patience, time, and effort. If partners put in the hard work to achieve recovery, they can work together in overcoming addiction.

Identifying Your Negative Voice

Jon, a fifty-four-year-old man, struggled with alcoholism. His thirty-five-year-old partner, Becca, couldn't understand his addiction. She came into the office and nearly burst into tears. "I just can't understand why he can't stop drinking! It's not that hard! Why can't he just stop? He just won't do it! Can't he see how many things he's ruined because of his drinking? I can't believe he relapsed again. He's lost jobs, money, and he's about to lose me, again!"

I understood Becca's frustration. It's hard being the partner of an addict. When a partner's addiction wreaks havoc on their lives, people feel powerless. It can be hard to see a partner relapsing over and over again, and continue to harm the relationship, without seeming to learn from their mistakes. We love our partner but hate their addiction.

However, it's difficult for those struggling with addiction to "just stop." There are a lot of misconceptions about addiction, and part of recovery involves educating ourselves with the correct information. Education can increase our compassion for people like Jon, who was experiencing a lot of shame for not being able to stop.

I talked about resources and recovery steps for both Jon and Becca. It's always important for both partners to seek treatment. In their case, recovery involved an immediate detox program for Jon, then individual therapy and group support for both partners, as well as tools to help each of them. Jon mentioned he was familiar with AA, but Becca had no idea a support group existed for people with addicted partners. Armed with information, tools, and support, the couple had a good plan in place.

After Jon finished his detox program, I saw the couple again, and I asked Jon about his inner dialogue.

"Jon, when you're feeling low, what are the thoughts that run through your head?"

Jon paused and said, "Um, probably something like I'm not good enough. I shouldn't exist. I'm a failure. Oh, and I suck. Yeah, the list pretty much sounds like that."

Indeed, those struggling with addiction typically experience low self-esteem and deep shame about their addiction, and this is often experienced in the form of a negative inner voice. Everyone has one but some are louder than others. I asked Jon to name his.

"Name it?" he said, laughing.

"Yes," I said.

"I'll call it Bob," he said. "Bob was this annoying guy at work."

If we name our negative voice, it allows us to distance ourselves from it. In other words, when we separate ourselves from our negative voice, we recognize that the voice is a remote part of us, not our complete self.

You can choose whatever name you want for your voice. For example, some people struggling with an eating disorder call their negative voice "ED," short for eating disorder. Some use humor and call it "That Guy" or "the Itty-Bitty Shitty Committee." The important thing is that the name is a reminder that this negative voice is just one aspect of our thoughts.

Jon explained to me and Becca what "Bob" represented to him.

"Bob," Jon said, "is my negative voice that tells me I'm no good. I'm not valuable. Bob wants me to fail. He doesn't believe in me."

Becca's face softened. "I get it," she said. "I actually have some of those thoughts, too. That I'm not pretty enough or that I can't do my job as well as my colleagues. I have a similar voice, too."

"Name it," I said.

"Elizabeth," Becca said. "She was this girl who in seventh grade made fun of my dance tryout. Urg. She didn't believe in me either."

I wanted Jon and Becca to share their voices to help unify them. It's helpful for all partners to share theirs with each other;

try it with your partner. It might feel awkward to share our name for this voice, but it's a helpful reminder to a partner that these negative thoughts aren't us and that we all struggle to be our best selves. Partners are in the recovery process together.

Finally, we have to learn how to let go of our negative voice. Every day, we each process over sixty thousand thoughts, and I asked Jon and Becca, "How many of them are negative?"

"A lot," they both said simultaneously.

That's true for many people, and we often forget we don't need to buy into each thought.

"For example," I said, "if someone cuts you off while driving, you may think, *I want to punch that driver*. But you don't, of course, you just think it. It was a negative thought you had, and chances are it passed rather quickly. The same goes for negative thoughts pertaining to addiction. You may think, *I am so depressed. The way to make me feel better is to overeat*. Or the partner of the addicted individual may think, *Oh no. I know he will relapse again and then I'll have to clean up the mess!* But we have to remember, these are just feelings, not facts. And feelings pass."

I gave them both a visual.

"It might be helpful to imagine writing that negative thought on a piece of paper. Next, visualize yourself crumbling that piece of paper with the words written down and throwing it in a river. Now imagine the thought floating down the river. The thought exists, but it's passing by. It's moving on. Or imagine a cartoon person with a thought bubble above their head thinking that negative thought. Now picture that thought bubble floating by them after they think it. It just slowly moves out of their view."

Visualizations can help us "see" that a thought is not permanent. They may feel like the truth at that moment, but they will pass, like all thoughts. We have the choice to engage in those thoughts or not.

Jon and Becca actively practiced not engaging in their negative thoughts. It took work, but over time, the couple told me it helped them to not take each thought so seriously. Jon was able to not buy into his thoughts about how he wasn't good enough, and Becca said it changed her work performance.

Negative voices can feel scary and real, and they play into addiction. We can use tools to help identify, name, and visualize them dissipating. This helps prevent relapse because it forces people to examine their thoughts. Thoughts can quickly become actions, and this process helps take back control of our thoughts.

It's challenging when a partner experiences an addiction, but with the right resources, patience, commitment, and support — along with understanding addiction, planning for recovery, and identifying negative voices — partners can navigate the recovery journey together.

"Things Are Different Since We Had Kids"

O ne of the most significant life changes we can experience is having children. Feelings about parenting often involve contradictory emotions. Depending on the day, we can experience feelings of joy, fatigue, frustration, excitement, loneliness, and fulfillment. Having children is also a major transition in a partnership. Adding a new member, or members, to the family is a huge dynamic shift. Starting a family is one of the most enriching experiences couples can go through, and it can also be one of the most challenging.

When couples start out, they only have their own needs to worry about. When they have a child, the child's needs become the priority, especially while they are an infant. This shifting of priorities can deeply affect a relationship.

It's OK for people to feel sad, angry, or defeated about how a relationship changes after children. It's understandable for partners to miss the time they had with just the two of them. Here are three strategies that can help partners reinvigorate their dynamic after having kids: experiencing the before, assessing your relationship post-kid(s), and creating a division of child responsibilities.

Experiencing the Before

It's important to incorporate some of what made a relationship exciting and fun before having a child but that might now feel lost. Partners should think about the types of things they enjoyed early in their romance: Was it outdoor activities, movies, traveling, or reading together? How, with a little modification, can they bring some of those things back? They won't be exactly as they were pre-kids, but it's possible to restore some of the goodness and joy they inspired.

Ross and Amanda were a couple in their late thirties who came to me because "things weren't the same after they had kids." They now had two boys, three and five years old. Both Ross and Amanda worked full-time, and they longed for the days they could just lounge around on the weekends doing whatever they wanted after a long workweek. Nowadays, they were busy with their kids: taking one son to soccer, the other to a playdate, giving baths, and handling tantrums. The new family dynamic was difficult for the couple to navigate.

Raising children is hard. One way it's hard is that a couple can't put the same time and attention into their romantic relationship. That can lead to feelings of grief, as the partners mourn the loss of the relationship and life they had pre-kids. They have more responsibility, less free time, and are often way more tired. Of course, kids are beautiful, and having kids can fulfill lifelong dreams, but that doesn't negate longing for what is now missing when a couple could focus all their love and attention on each other. That's OK. Both feelings can exist: sadness about the old dynamic and happiness about the new one.

In our society, there is a taboo about prioritizing a romantic relationship after a couple has children. I believe we have to honor both: our relationship with our partner and the relationship with our family and kids. They may not be equally balanced all the time, but it's important we give attention to both.

I asked Ross and Amanda about their life before kids. They

both lit up. "Oh, we loved to have picnics in the park," Amanda said.

"And remember we'd binge-watch a Netflix series?" Ross said.

"Yes," Amanda sighed. "Those were the days!"

I asked the couple if they ever did either of those things with the kids. They looked surprised. "With our kids?" they asked.

"Yes," I said. "What if you had a picnic with the kids in the park? And afterward, what if you watched a child-friendly movie or cartoon together? Of course, it won't be the same, but the idea is still there."

They agreed to try, and to their amazement, it worked out pretty well.

"It wasn't the same as just us," Ross said. "But better than I thought! I forgot how much I missed some of those things we used to do."

I wanted Ross and Amanda to honor both: their life as partners and their life as a family. I asked them to schedule romantic date nights (see "Date Nights and Scheduling," page 28) as well as do things as a family that they missed from when they dated. A few weeks later Amanda told me they cooked as a family because one of their favorite dates included cooking together. Amanda bought their youngest a baby utensil set, and he was able to use his ladle to stir the bowl. Ross said he helped the oldest pour in the ingredients.

Parents can get very focused on their kids' activities and forget about including their kids in the activities they like. As Amanda and Ross did more of the things that they liked with their kids, their life began to feel a bit more balanced and entertaining.

It's beneficial to do activities that you used to do with your partner with your new family. It might take a little creativity to figure out how to achieve it, but it can make the days more enjoyable and memorable.

Here are some ideas:

- If you loved to hike with your partner, do a family hike. With an infant, utilize a backpack. Or if your child is bigger and can walk, play a scavenger hunt with them to find things along the way.
- If you were into gardening, visit an arboretum with the family. Or purchase a grow-your-own-garden kit, and teach the kids how to plant seeds.
- If you liked adventure as a couple, take kids overnight camping, go geocaching, or even have an "adventure" at a theme park. Take a surprise drive to some place you've never been.
- If you were into movies, go to a fun drive-in movie theater with the kids, a 4D movie, or have the kids set up their own popcorn stand and projector. If the kids are old enough, they can take the tickets and usher you to your seats.
- If you were into crafting, create a photo album. Kids love looking at pictures of themselves, and they can pick the ones they like best.
- If you did a lot of outdoor sports, go to a family rock climbing center, play Frisbee, or build a labyrinth.
- If you both like to read, write a family story together, read stories to the kids, or play Mad Libs.
- If you loved escape rooms, create your own escape-room mystery game, one suitable for your kids, or create your own board game together.
- If you loved being silly, be silly! Draw funny faces on water balloons or play charades.

- If you loved to bowl, create an indoor bowling alley by using plastic bottles or paper towel rolls as "pins" and toilet paper rolls or tennis balls as bowling balls.

Incorporating the activities you liked as a couple has two advantages. First, it allows you to experience what you previously enjoyed, which brings back fond memories. Second, it also enables you to start new traditions with the family, which creates new memories.

If partners struggle with this even after their kids have grown and left the house, see Issue 3: "We Don't Make Time for Each Other" (page 27).

Assessing Your Relationship Post-Kid(s)

When partners take on their new roles as parents, they often can't anticipate all the many ways their lives will change after having children. These new roles are very different and change the dynamic in their relationship. It's important to address these changes to improve their relationship.

To start, partners need to have an open and honest conversation about their relationship after having kids. If you are doing this with your partner, utilize the chart below as a reference. Create your own version and feel free to add more topics. Or you can download a blank version of this chart from my website, KelliMillerTherapy.com. Talk to each other candidly. What is currently working or not working in the relationship? What feels different or needs improvement? With each particular topic, both partners should write down their feelings before and after kids, and then together they can come up with a solution on how to address each issue. This is not a time for blame; the goal is to unify and seek solutions for making the relationship better.

Post-Kid(s) Relationship Assessment			
Topic	*Before Kids*	*After Kids*	*Solution*
Communication	*Felt strong and consistent.*	*Feels difficult to talk due to lack of time.*	Set aside weekly time to talk, or plan a family meeting weekly.
Time management	*Felt OK.*	*Feels like we have no time.*	Create a joint schedule or calendar. Prioritize a list of most-important things to get done daily.
Work schedule	*Felt difficult but manageable.*	*Feels overwhelming and exhausting.*	Help each other with ways to make the work schedule easier. Delegate tasks to others. Make a list of things accomplished and celebrate successes.
Routine	*Felt solid.*	*Feels hard because of the changing needs of kids.*	Keep a tentative routine but be flexible; schedules with kids often vary.
Responsibilities	*Felt we did a good job working together.*	*Feels unequal at times.*	See "Division of Child Responsibilities" (page 131).

Priorities	Felt manageable because it was just us.	The kids are now a priority.	Create a better balance with your kids' needs and your own, such as with more self-care and date nights.
Social life	Felt good and we went out with our friends often.	We need more social plans with friends. Hard with kids.	Make more plans to go out with friends, with or without the children.
Finances	Felt OK.	Worry about money more.	Consider talking to a financial planner; see Issue 9: "We Spend Money Differently" (page 99).
Emotional changes	Felt happy.	Feel more anxious, stressed, and overwhelmed.	Think about speaking to a licensed therapist or joining a support group for new parents.
Sex life	Felt consistent and adventurous.	Feels inconsistent and boring.	See Issue 4: "We Don't Have Sex Anymore" (page 39).

There are many ways to adjust to new roles and expectations. If we can add in structure and creativity, we can feel more on the same page with our partners. Consider the following:

- **Have a weekly family meeting to set expectations:** Consistent family meetings can provide partners the space to talk about parenting issues as well as the relationship. Depending on the ages of the children, encourage them to participate as well. Including children can foster a sense of inclusiveness and collaboration.

- **Create a family vision board:** Partners can sit down together, and/or with children, and create an inspiration board that represents everyone's shared goals, dreams, and aspirations, both for the family and the relationship. Use cutouts from magazines, printed drawings, or images to visually represent everyone's vision. This can be a fun and creative way to get excited about the future.

- **Brainstorm a bucket list of relationship and family activities:** What do you still dream of doing, both together as a couple and as a family? For example, one item can be for a romantic getaway and another might be a family trip to Disney World. Having something to look forward to will help when things feel chaotic and difficult.

- **Create a gratitude jar:** Studies show writing down what we appreciate can make us happier. Have the kids design the "gratitude jar," and then have everyone write down the things they are grateful for. The sky's the limit for expressing gratitude: include people, places, things, feelings, anything. There are also no limits on how many gratitude notes can be placed in the jar. Read the notes during family meetings or when times are especially tough. Focusing on what we are grateful for can remind us of things that are working in our lives and can strengthen the bond within a family.

We have to be proactive in our relationship after having children. That means having clear and honest conversations as well as incorporating creative ideas that work for the family. In doing so, we can continue to build a fulfilling partnership even amid the changes of parenthood.

Division of Child Responsibilities

Having children can alter priorities and responsibilities. We feel more pressure to fulfill our parenting duties. People can sometimes make unspoken assumptions about what a partner might do regarding specific tasks, which might relate to un-shared ideas about traditional gender roles. Whether partners fulfill assumptions or not, there can be a strain on the relationship.

The first step to setting up a new life after kids is for partners to be patient and compassionate with each other. Each person's life has changed, and there is now added stress. Some partners may adjust better, while others struggle with new roles, responsibilities, and time management. Patience is vital as partners navigate this new phase of their relationship.

Second, partners need to consider the impact of their respective upbringings. In other words, it's helpful for partners to understand how their lives as children, and the roles their parents or caregivers played, impact their feelings about parenting. We don't always realize how much our own childhood experiences factor into our current lives. Partners should talk openly about their childhoods to understand more about how this impacts their current situation.

Important questions to ask are: What roles did parents play? Who took care of the kids? Who worked? In two-parent families, was it a traditional dynamic? In divorced families, how did the parenting responsibilities differ? In a single-parent household, how were responsibilities managed? Did individual parents assume certain expectations? Partners should listen gently to each other's answers and talk about how their upbringings have influenced their parenting.

Third, consider creating more structure via a parenting chart. Establishing expectations and roles helps ward off resentment because responsibilities are clearly defined. Similar to a chore chart (see "Chore Chart," page 69), a parenting chart helps ensure that parenting tasks are evenly distributed.

To create a chart, partners should discuss their individual strengths, preferences, and schedules. For example, in regard to strengths: Is one person more tolerant with homework help, while the other feels more confident giving baths? In regard to preferences, does one prefer to pick up the kids while the other prefers to prepare dinner? In regard to schedules, is it more convenient for one parent to pick up the kids because daycare is closer to their work?

Using those strengths, preferences, and schedules, create a parenting chart similar to the one on the next page, or download a blank template from my website, KelliMillerTherapy.com.

Parenting Task Chart			
Day of Week	*Parenting Task*	*Week 1*	*Week 2*
Monday	Wash bottles	Partner 1	Partner 2
Tuesday	Take child to soccer	Partner 2	Partner 1
Wednesday	Prepare dinner	Partner 1	Partner 2
Thursday	Do home-work	Partner 2	Partner 1
Friday	Pick up kids from school	Partner 1	Partner 2
Saturday	Bath time	Partner 2	Partner 1
Sunday	Sort laundry	Partner 1	Partner 2

Remember, a parenting chart should be flexible and account for changes. Life brings us many surprises, which can affect our schedule and routines. For example, if one partner agrees to take the kids to school every day, but that partner gets pulled into a regular morning meeting, partners can switch tasks. Or if soccer practice moves to a different day that works better with the other partner's schedule, adjust. Remember, the goal is for partners to work as a unit and help each other.

If childhood tasks remain difficult to manage and are straining a relationship, consider seeking outside help. Involve grandparents, neighbors, or friends, which is a great way to help offset some responsibilities. If family or friends aren't an option, be creative: Hire a babysitter, a nanny, housecleaners, or a local high school or college student on days when things are especially hard.

Being compassionate with our partner, understanding how our partner grew up in their household, and generating a parenting chart will help with the division of child responsibilities. There can be a lot of misunderstandings or assumptions about parenting roles. If we can get clarity by establishing more parental organization, we can feel more solidified as parents and partners.

Having children is a significant life change that impacts relationships, but you can strengthen your partnership and navigate these changes together by experiencing the before, assessing your relationship post-kid(s), and dividing child responsibilities.

ISSUE 12

"I Don't Feel Respected by My Partner"

Feeling respected is paramount to a relationship. If we feel respected by our partners, we feel loved and appreciated. Conversely, if we don't feel respected, we feel unloved and unappreciated. In order to have a fulfilling and secure relationship, both partners should actively strive to appreciate each other's feelings, opinions, and boundaries.

Respect for our partners comes in three equally important parts: an appreciation for who the other person is and/or what they have achieved, treating them in a dignified way, and understanding their right to self-determination. In other words, respect in a relationship involves deep admiration for the other, speaking and behaving in kind ways, and acknowledging the other's feelings, needs, opinions, and boundaries. The three pieces of respect foster a positive and supportive partnership and promote security within a relationship.

Conversely, disrespectful behavior and language damage a relationship as well as the other person's sense of well-being. Disrespect in a relationship is showing a lack of regard and consideration, and this can include using derogatory language, condescending behavior, controlling or manipulative behavior, and/or crossing physical or emotional boundaries. The important thing is that both partners feel safe and respected in the relationship.

Disrespect can also lead to abuse, and if you feel this is the case for you, it's important to take steps to protect yourself. Abuse involves cruelty, mistreatment, and/or violence, and it can be physical, emotional, verbal, psychological, financial, digital, or sexual. Awareness of abusive behavior is the first step to dealing with it. If you sense something is wrong, please do not doubt yourself and immediately prioritize your safety and well-being. This can include creating a safety plan (figuring out a safe place to go as well as gathering important belongings), calling the police, seeking professional help, and developing a support system.

For more information, contact these hotlines:

National Domestic Violence Hotline (800-799-7233, www.thehotline.org)
National Sexual Assault Hotline (800-656-4673, www.rainn.org)

To build a healthier partnership, it's important for people to address any feelings of disrespect. Respect is crucial to relationships to build mutual trust, intimacy, and security. In this chapter, I offer three tools: using BISECT, understanding cognitive distortions, and following respect initiatives that identify the source of issues and then playing "games" that help develop reverence.

BISECT: A Way to Show Respect

Respect can come in many forms. The acronym I created to remind partners about what is important in a relationship is BISECT, which stands for boundaries, independence, support, equality, communication, and trust. If partners can take the time to understand and practice each form, this can contribute to a more intimate, trusting, and understanding relationship.

Boundaries

Respecting our partner's boundaries entails honoring their needs, personal space, and privacy. We want to encourage open discussions about what feels safe and comfortable in the relationship. For example, this might be asking to not have public displays of affection or using a softer voice when arguing. We create boundaries with our partners in order to feel secure and structured within the relationship. For more about boundaries, see "Understanding the Affair and Setting Boundaries" (page 86).

Independence

Autonomy within a relationship is not only necessary but essential. Giving our partners freedom to make their own decisions and have their own life outside of the relationship elicits trust within the partnership. When we give our partners the space and liberty to be who they are, they don't fear losing a part of themselves. In fact, they typically feel more connected to the partnership.

Support

Supporting our partners is a form of safety within the relationship. If we can support our partner's personal development goals, dreams, career, wants, and needs, we are respecting our partner for who they are. In challenging times, supporting our partner shows kindness and empathy and ultimately displays a deep respect for what they need.

Equality

We want to strive for a balanced relationship, which starts with equality. Equality is viewing our partners as an equal regardless of sex, race, religion, income level, or other differences.

Equality means seeing the relationship as an opportunity to value mutual responsibilities and decision making as well as striving for an equal power dynamic.

Communication

Effective communication is the hallmark of a secure relationship. It's essential that partners learn the skills and tools to talk with each other about their needs, boundaries, fears, and frustrations. Respecting our partners in communication involves actively listening to our partners, watching our tone and volume when getting heated, using appropriate language, and being honest. For more on communication, see Issue 1: "My Partner Doesn't Listen to Me" (page 5).

Trust

Trust starts with being honest and transparent with our partners. If we are reliable and consistent in what we say and do, our partners will feel more secure in our relationship. For more about building trust, see Issue 7: "We Can't Trust Each Other after Infidelity" (page 77).

Feeling respected in a partnership makes a difference in the quality and fulfillment of our relationships. Actively using BISECT will help partners feel more valued, appreciated, and respected.

Cognitive Distortions

Most of our thoughts are conscious, but some aren't. And those unconscious thoughts can sometimes lead us to negative thinking about our partners. These defeatist thoughts are called cognitive distortions. Cognitive distortions are patterns of thinking that can be biased, inaccurate, and lead us to dangerous generalizations. Examples include "I'm such a loser for making a mistake" or "I feel anxious about presenting my project at work, so I must be incompetent." These distortions can influence our emotions and behaviors surrounding our partners and the relationship. Since we are unaware of these thoughts, we may not even realize we are having them nor how they are impacting our partnership. It's helpful to become aware of cognitive distortions so we can recognize how they can impact our relationship.

Here are some of the most common cognitive distortions:

All-or-nothing thinking: This means seeing things in absolute terms without recognizing the possibility of a middle ground. For example, thinking that if our partner disagrees with us on a certain issue, we're incompatible and the relationship is doomed.

Overgeneralization: This is drawing broad conclusions from one single event or a limited set of experiences. For example, assuming that because our partner forgot to pick up the milk one time, they will always forget to pick up the milk.

Catastrophizing: Magnifying the severity of a situation and then imagining the worst possible outcome is catastrophizing. For example, assuming that because our spouse forgot to get an anniversary gift, they no longer love us and want a divorce.

Emotional reasoning: This means believing that our feelings and emotions are true facts, without considering evidence to the contrary. For example, assuming that because we feel anxious in the relationship, something must be actually wrong in the relationship.

Jumping to conclusions: Also called mind reading, this is assuming that we know what others are thinking or feeling without evidence. For example, believing that our partner is angry with us without asking them if this is actually true.

Personalization: This is taking responsibility for events or situations that are beyond our control. For example, if someone planned to go out with their partner on a night when it snowed, forcing them to cancel the date, the person would feel it was their fault because they picked that date and time.

Discounting positives: This means focusing only on the negative and ignoring the positive. For example, if a partner expresses appreciation for being served breakfast in bed but mentions that the coffee got cold, the person would only focus on what wasn't perfect.

"Should" statements: This is when using words like *should*, *must*, or *ought to* indicate someone has unrealistic expectations. For example, thinking that our partner *should* act in different ways if they really loved us.

Labeling: Labels take one characteristic and generalize it, so that it applies to the whole person. For example, if a partner is frequently late to work, calling them "irresponsible."

Becoming Aware of Cognitive Distortions

If we can recognize and become aware of any cognitive distortions, we can challenge and correct them, and this can improve our relationship. As an example, consider Rick and Maria.

Rick and Maria were a couple in their late fifties. Both were exhibiting cognitive distortions about the other without realizing it, and these distortions had led to disrespect toward each other.

The couple's twenty-fifth anniversary was coming up. Maria had an engraved ring made for Rick, while Rick forgot to get Maria a gift, and they got into an argument in my office. Below, I name their cognitive distortions in brackets.

Maria said, "Since you forgot about my gift, you must not love me *[jumping to conclusions]*. You'll just continue to forget our big events *[overgeneralization]*. It will always be this bad *[all-or-nothing thinking]*. I know we are going to get a divorce *[catastrophizing]*."

Rick replied, "You should always remind me the week before *["should" statement]*! Since I messed up this anniversary, we are clearly not meant to be, and clearly should get a divorce *[all-or-nothing thinking]*!"

I helped Rick and Maria see how they both were using cognitive distortions without even realizing it. As they became more conscious of these distortions, they were able to speak more respectfully to each other, since they started using language that was less emotional and more neutral.

Recognizing and confronting cognitive distortions can be an important part of recognizing our own unconscious thoughts and mindset. If we can be more aware of our generalizations, we can ultimately be more respectful of our partners.

Respect Initiatives

Like trust, respect in a relationship needs to be earned. Earning the respect of a partner is important because it improves trust, intimacy, and communication.

There are many things partners can do to earn respect. Most important is treating the other person with love and appreciation and a recognition of their self-determination. But sometimes partners don't feel respected or act in respectful ways because they feel angry or resentful. When this is the case, partners need to examine why they are feeling resentful. After that is uncovered, they can focus on activities and games that increase appreciation for their partner.

Exploring Resentments

Each partner needs to pinpoint the cause of their feelings, whether they are experiencing a lack of respect from their partner or find it hard to be respectful toward the other. In what situations do these feelings arise? Is there something specific the couple can address to help improve these situations? One example might be when one person is talking with friends, and the other person often interrupts to tell their version of a story. The person being interrupted might feel undermined or disrespected. If so, the couple needs to have an open dialogue about this.

The partner who is upset might say something along these lines:

> I really value our relationship, and I love when we go out with our friends together. But I feel upset when I start telling a story and you interrupt to tell your story. You may not realize you're doing this, and I don't think you mean to be disrespectful, but that's how I feel in the moment. It would mean a lot to me if I could finish my story with friends before you tell yours.

Often, partners don't realize the impact of their actions, and they don't intend to cause upset. Meanwhile, one person is fuming and not saying anything, and the same scenario keeps happening. It's essential we bring up difficult topics to mend the relationship. For more on having a healthy dialogue, see Issue 1: "My Partner Doesn't Listen to Me" (page 5).

Alternatively, one partner might be carrying an unconscious resentment. They might feel angry about a past hurt, and it's causing them to treat their partner with disrespect. For more on identifying and handling resentment, see "Looking at Resentments" (page 40).

Games for Rebuilding Respect and Admiration

After couples sort through understanding why they feel a lack of respect and resentment, they can focus on rebuilding their appreciation, admiration, and respect for each other. Here are a few unconventional ways to do that.

> **The Respect Scavenger Hunt:** Each partner writes ten notes about what they respect about their partner. This could be things like a partner's work ethic, their ability to speak to a stranger, or how they wake up motivated for the day. Both partners hide the notes through their home and give clues to their partner on where they are placed. Opening and finding the notes reinforces positive affirmations and reminds us why we are respected by our partners.

> **The Conflict Resolution Game:** Choose a hypothetical conflict or a current one in the news. For example, if a celebrity spoke rudely to a fan or a high-powered politician proposed controversial legislation. As a team, the couple can discuss how they would handle the problem. If they were that celebrity, would they apologize? If they were the politician, how would they handle the controversy?

Collaboratively finding solutions can strengthen the respect and trust in the relationship.

The Transformation Game: Partners can swap roles for a day. For example, if one partner typically handles the majority of the childcare, let the other partner take over those responsibilities. Or if one partner typically does the laundry each week, have the other partner do the laundry for a week. This game allows each partner to experience and appreciate the other's responsibilities and contributions, which promotes empathy and understanding in the relationship.

Talking-Stick Conversations: In group discussions, the person holding the "talking stick" is the only one allowed to speak. Partners can use this practice to help foster attentiveness and active listening, which are key components of respect. Any item can be used as a "talking stick." Whichever partner has the stick can speak, while the other partner listens. The speaker can share their thoughts or feelings about anything, and the listener can practice active listening by asking questions or repeating what their partner has said to confirm understanding. Then partners switch roles.

The Great Divide Game: Healthy relationships require respecting each other's boundaries. Partners can challenge each other to see if they know their personal boundaries. Each should state where they feel the other stands on personal space, alone time, physical and emotional boundaries, and so on. Reinforcing each other's boundaries is a good reminder on what feels safe in the relationship.

Escapades and Adventures: Partners can plan an outing or adventure that pushes them both out of their comfort zones. Explore a new town, try a new outdoor activity like kayaking or pickleball, or take a road trip. Trying something new with a partner can help strengthen bonds and create new memories.

Recollections and Shared Memories: Reminiscing about favorite memories together is a great way for couples to respect their shared history. Look at old photos, watch videos, and talk about favorite past experiences. Experiencing nostalgia can bring back feelings of appreciation between partners.

The Story Game: Write a creative story together. Determine the premise or plot, and then each person can switch off writing. Perhaps switch every paragraph, every sentence, or every half sentence. This encourages mutual respect for each other's ideas, creativity, and imagination.

The Tribute Game: Take turns giving each other authentic compliments. Compliments can be focused on emotional, physical, or spiritual qualities. This game encourages positive reinforcement and helps both partners feel seen, valued, and respected for who they are.

The Gratitude Game: Partners can take turns expressing appreciation and gratitude for everything in their lives: their physical surroundings, dwelling, kids, pets, jobs, and anything they value. This game encourages partners to consciously appreciate what they have together as well as cultivate gratitude and respect for each other.

The Amnesty Game: Practice forgiveness by taking

turns apologizing for any past hurts, mistakes, or misunderstandings. This game is a way for partners to show respect to each other by being vulnerable, understanding, and acknowledging their partner's humanity.

Uncovering the reasons why we aren't feeling appreciated and discussing it with our partner is a key component of creating a more respectful relationship. Then we can move forward and rebuild respect directly by fostering continual appreciation of each other.

There are many keys to creating a satisfying, secure, and happy relationship. Two main components are respect and appreciation. To help foster these, we can use BISECT, understand any cognitive distortions, and pursue respect initiatives.

ISSUE 13

"Social Media Is Damaging Our Relationship"

I n today's world, we can't escape social media. Everywhere we look there are websites, apps, and digital channels connecting people all over the world. We can share thoughts, information, and even build, form, and maintain friendships with people in ways we were never able to before. Social media has fundamentally changed our lives.

While there are many positives of social media, there are also a lot of downsides. Concerns over privacy, miscommunications, comparisons that spark jealousy, and cyberbullying are some of the ways that social media can impact us negatively.

Both positively and negatively, social media can also impact our romantic relationships. Some romances start via online connections, but they can end that way, too, such as when one person reconnects with an ex-partner and starts to "cheat" online. Or if one or both partners spend too much time online, leading to constant arguments. Whatever the case, couples have to find the appropriate boundaries of social media use in their relationship.

If social media is affecting your relationship, it's vital to start by filling out the questionnaire on social media on the following pages, then establish social media boundaries and explore the practice I call "using the mirror on why."

Questionnaire on Social Media

Social media platforms are designed to be addictive. The constant stimulation and gratification make it difficult to stop. If not used in moderation, social media can be a form of obsession. If social media use is impacting a relationship, it's important for partners to first gauge their usage and its influence or impact on their partnership. This questionnaire is designed to do just that.

Each partner should fill out this questionnaire separately, and you can download it from my website, KelliMillerTherapy.com:

1. How often do you use social media platforms such as Instagram, TikTok, Facebook, or X (formally known as Twitter)?
   a. Several times a day
   b. Once a day
   c. A few times a week
   d. Rarely or never
2. How often has your partner asked you questions and you didn't respond because you were too busy looking at social media?
   a. Often
   b. Sometimes
   c. Rarely
   d. Never
3. Have you ever felt like your use of social media has interfered with your ability to communicate productively?
   a. Yes, often
   b. Yes, sometimes
   c. Rarely
   d. Never

4. When using social media, how often do you find yourself comparing your partner or relationship to others on social media?
   a. Often
   b. Sometimes
   c. Rarely
   d. Never

5. When using social media, how often do you find yourself feeling insecure, jealous, or angry about your partner's interactions with others on social media?
   a. Often
   b. Sometimes
   c. Rarely
   d. Never

6. How often do you feel tempted to engage or talk with someone you know your partner wouldn't approve of on social media?
   a. Often
   b. Sometimes
   c. Rarely
   d. Never

7. How often do you find yourself arguing with your partner about their social media use?
   a. Often
   b. Sometimes
   c. Rarely
   d. Never

8. Have you ever felt like your partner is hiding or withholding something from you in their social media interactions?
   a. Yes, often
   b. Yes, sometimes

    c. Rarely

    d. Never

9. How often do you feel like your partner is more invested in their social media relationships than in your relationship?

    a. Often

    b. Sometimes

    c. Rarely

    d. Never

10. Have you ever felt like your partner is spending too much time on social media and consequently not enough time with you?

    a. Yes, often

    b. Yes, sometimes

    c. Rarely

    d. Never

11. How often do you find yourself feeling unsatisfied, unfulfilled, or unsettled in your relationship due to social media use?

    a. Often

    b. Sometimes

    c. Rarely

    d. Never

12. How often do you feel like social media causes miscommunication, misunderstandings, or misinterpretations in your relationship?

    a. Often

    b. Sometimes

    c. Rarely

    d. Never

13. How often do you feel like you or your partner's social media use has negatively impacted your emotional or sexual intimacy?

  a. Often
  b. Sometimes
  c. Rarely
  d. Never
14. Have you ever felt like your partner's social media use has caused you to question the honesty in your relationship?
  a. Yes, often
  b. Yes, sometimes
  c. Rarely
  d. Never
15. How often do you feel like your partner's social media use has made you feel less valued in your relationship?
  a. Often
  b. Sometimes
  c. Rarely
  d. Never

This questionnaire is designed to encourage conversation about the impact of social media use. There is no right answer or definitive scoring. This questionnaire is more of a self-examination exercise to encourage open and honest conversations. Partners should talk about their answers and what they uncover. If partners determine that social media is affecting their relationship, establishing social media boundaries is the next step.

Establishing Social Media Boundaries

If social media use is impacting a relationship, it's important for partners to establish boundaries surrounding privacy, time spent online, and engagement on social media. Boundaries are not a means to control or punish either partner; rather, they are ways to establish trust, security, and respect in the relationship. For more about boundaries, see "Setting Boundaries" (page 88).

To initiate a conversation about social media use, you can say something like this:

I really value our relationship, and I love spending time with you. I've noticed that social media is affecting our relationship. Can we please talk about some boundaries that work for us?

Partners can then use the following topics and suggestions as a way to establish limits and comfort levels for both people. If partners have differing views, what's important is being flexible and understanding and finding a reasonable compromise that will work for both people. For more on negotiating compromises that feel comfortable and respectful, see "Who Is More Emotionally Invested?" (page 22).

Partners should first answer the following questions separately in their journal, and then afterward discuss their answers together and utilize any suggestions they agree with.

Topic: Social Media Privacy

QUESTIONS

1. What does privacy mean to you in regard to social media?
2. Are you a private person who would rather keep their personal life private and not online?
3. Are you OK if your life is more public?
4. How do you feel if your partner posts words or photos about your relationship?

SUGGESTIONS

Set some ground rules. Define what works for both partners in regard to privacy. For example, perhaps this means asking each other before posting something or avoiding posting particular photos or certain topics. Consider the long-term effects. Have a discussion about whether posting helps or hinders the relationship. Examine whether both partners would feel comfortable with a particular post years from now.

Topic: Account Privacy

QUESTIONS

1. How do you feel about keeping your accounts and messages private from one another?
2. Would you want free rein to see each other's social media accounts?

SUGGESTIONS

Have an honest conversation about account privacy and why each person feels the way they do. It might be helpful to explain differences, such as if one partner wants to keep their account private and the other wants to share theirs. Compromise. If partners disagree about account accessibility, is there a middle ground? For example, are there certain aspects of a partner's social media account that are OK to view when together?

Topic: Time Online

QUESTION

1. How much time on social media feels respectful to your partnership?

SUGGESTIONS

Settle on timing together. If one partner wants to be on social media five times a day and the other doesn't want any social media, consider one to two times a day as a halfway point. Establish a "social media–free zone" during certain times of the day. Agree to put computers and phones away while partners focus on each other. This can be during dinnertime or date nights.

Topic: Engagement

QUESTIONS

1. How do you feel about engaging with followers or influencers?
2. How do you feel about partners connecting with ex-partners?
3. What defines appropriate engagement with people online?

SUGGESTIONS

Establish a follow and no-follow list together. Agree on a mutual list of people acceptable for both partners to follow or not follow, as well as what constitutes appropriate communication with them. Setting guidelines on who is acceptable will clear up misunderstandings later on down the line. Create a joint social media account. Setting up a joint social media account will create a sense of transparency in a relationship, and partners both have access to followers and conversations.

Remember, it's important to be honest about what you need in order to feel comfortable. Every relationship is unique, and it's important to figure out a solution that works for both partners. Generating boundaries around social media can give the partnership clear guidelines and make the partnership a safer one.

Using the Mirror on Why

"Using the mirror on why" refers to examining why we do certain things. It requires a level of honesty and self-awareness. It's not about judgment or shame over why we do these things. Rather, it seeks to understand and interpret behaviors. It's an emotional deep dive into acknowledging our actions.

Thirty-five-year-old Kwame and twenty-three-year-old Dami came to me because they felt social media was affecting their relationship. Kwame was a project manager at a technology company, and Dami was a social media influencer. Kwame felt Dami's life revolved around social media. Dami insisted she had to be on social media for her job. I asked Dami to "use the mirror on why" related to her social media use separate from work.

Dami admitted that, when her friends posted online, she had a deep level of FOMO, or fear of missing out. Dami felt looking at her social media made her feel a level of connection to others, even if she couldn't be present personally. It made her feel that she was "in the know" about what everyone was up to and where they were physically.

I applauded Dami's honesty and self-reflection and reassured she was not alone. Many people have a fear of missing out on important events. There is a pull to stay constantly connected with friends and family and a curiosity to see what people are doing, especially if we aren't with them.

Although Kwame appreciated Dami's honesty, he wanted to know separately why she also felt the need to post pictures of herself all the time. Dami looked a bit embarrassed when Kwame said this, and she confessed that she liked the validation she received from both men and women from her posts. She said that receiving likes was almost like a "hit" to her.

Once again, Dami is not alone. Social media provides a stage to receive attention and validation. There can be a sense of competition to receive the most likes and comments among friends and others. These reactions make us feel good because our responses release dopamine, the hormone associated with pleasure and reward. Dopamine is the same neurotransmitter that is released when someone is gambling, so it is no wonder Dami felt it was like a "hit." The hormone feels so good people can get addicted to the behavior. In this case, Dami may have started to become addicted to social media. If you worry that you and your partner's social media use is teetering on addiction, see Issue 10: "My Partner or I Have an Addiction" (page 111).

Tearing up and feeling ashamed, Dami also admitted to using social media as an escape. Like millions of others, using social media can be a form of escapism to break away from life stressors. Social media can be a great distraction or entertainment when we want to avoid work, difficult feelings, or problems. In this case, Dami used social media to avoid feeling sad or lonely.

I suggested that Dami limit her social media use, especially when she was spending quality time with Kwame. I also asked her to consider more frequent in-person encounters with her friends in order to not feel left out. Next, I asked her to reflect on what she was feeling during the times she turned to social media and had the urge to post. In the moments before she was scrolling on her phone, could she check in to see what she was feeling? I also suggested Dami turn off alerts from her favorite apps, or at the very least she could place her phone on "do not disturb" so she wasn't constantly getting pinged with notifications. Finally, we set up a plan for alternate activities — like taking a walk, reading a book, or calling a friend — if she was feeling any uncomfortable feelings.

Here is a chart that can help you or your partner if social media is being overused. You can download a blank version of this chart for your own use from my website, KelliMiller Therapy.com.

Using the Mirror on Why			
What am I feeling right now?	What am I trying to gain?	What am I trying to escape?	What else can I do instead?
Sad	*Attention/ validation*	*Loneliness*	*Take a walk, read a book, call a friend*
Angry	*Redemption*	*Feeling un- comfortable*	*Take a kick- boxing class, journal, scream into a pillow*

Using the mirror on why is an excellent exercise to understand why we are doing certain things, such as overusing social media. If we can be truly honest with ourselves, we can use that self-examination and reflection to understand why we are doing certain behaviors. This awareness can lead us into helpful action, like limiting social media use.

We live in a technology-driven world. Disagreements about social media use are common among relationships. Completing the questionnaire on social media, establishing social media boundaries, and using the mirror on why will all help create clear structure and guidelines if social media is an issue in your relationship.

ISSUE 14

"We Want Different Things"

As humans, we all have certain needs and wants. A need is something essential and necessary for us to live. Having adequate shelter and enough food are needs. Conversely, wants are things we'd like to have that improve our quality of life. A bigger home or a new car are usually wants.

In childhood, we need to be cared for in order to thrive, and all people need housing, food, water, and clothing. Our wants aren't as essential as needs, and they typically shift over time as we develop preferences. In childhood, these wants can include things like playing certain sports, wearing certain clothes, and taking particular classes. Later, we recognize our wants in friendships and relationships. All people need friends and a supportive community, but each of us also wants friends and partners who possess certain qualities, like loyalty, humor, or even a little adventurousness, where we can take risks together.

It's natural to develop preferences and wants. These reflect our proclivities and personalities and what we've determined works best for us. In regard to partnerships, we have another set of needs and wants. Our needs are essential elements for the relationship to work, which are things like honesty and faithfulness. Wants may include things like having a partner who is a good cook or tidy.

What's difficult is when the needs and wants of partners clash. These differences may be present at the beginning of a relationship or they may develop over time. For example, at first, both partners might work and be pursuing careers, but after having children, due to their financial situation, one partner might need to stay home to care for the kids (even if they still want to work). Or perhaps when a couple was first dating, they both loved being social with friends, but over time, one partner came to prefer more nights with just their partner. Is being less social a want or a need? It depends, but recognizing differences and making these distinctions is essential. Doing so means communicating and bridging gaps to establish joint needs and wants.

I've developed several exercises to help couples better align their values: determining our needs from wants, unifying goals and dreams, and creating a values pie chart. These three tactics are all different ways of understanding what we need in our relationship and how to communicate those requirements going forward.

Just as our needs and wants may differ from one another, our processing of information can also vary. Some activities may be better suited for those who learn visually, and some exercises fit better with those who resonate with auditory activities. There is no obligation to try all the activities below. Choose what works best for you and your partner, or make an agreement that you each get to choose one.

Determining Our Needs from Wants

It's easy to get our needs and wants mixed up. Sometimes preferences feel so strong, it's hard to differentiate between the two. The way to look at needs and wants in a relationship is to determine the must-haves (needs) and the like-to-haves (wants). It's also essential to consider whether our needs and wants have changed over time.

To evaluate needs from wants, each partner should fill out a chart like the one below separately. If using the same chart, each person should use a different color pen in order to differentiate. You can download a blank version of this chart on my website, KelliMillerTherapy.com.

For each category, put a checkmark in either the Needs or Wants column, and then write a sentence briefly describing why it's a need or a want. For example, if someone marked "honesty" as a need, they might write something like, "I *need* to trust my partner in order to feel safe in the relationship." Or if they identified "sense of humor" as a want, they might write, "I *want* a partner who makes me laugh because it makes my day easier." Again, needs should feel essential, whereas wants feel more optional.

After each person fills out their wants and needs, they should discuss their choices, both the ones they agree on and the ones they differ on. It's understandable when partners have differing wants and needs in a relationship. What is most important is hearing each other's point of view and determining a compromise that satisfies what each person is looking for. For help reaching a compromise, see "Who Is More Emotionally Invested?" (page 22). Determining our wants from our needs helps avoid conflict with our partner over different priorities.

Needs and Wants			
Category	*Need*	*Want*	*Reason*
Honesty			
Loyalty			
Commitment			

Needs and Wants (*continued*)			
Category	*Need*	*Want*	*Reason*
Kindness			
Sense of humor			
Determination			
Strong work ethic			
Solid communication			
Emotional connection			
Equality in the relationship			
Empathy and understanding			
Date nights			
Quality time together			
Sexual intimacy and physical affection			
Shared interest in having children or expanding current family			
Mutual interests in hobbies or activities			
Emotional support			
Compatibility in values			
Shared household responsibilities/chores			
Romantic gestures			
Sense of adventure			

Physical and emotional safety			
Growth mindset			
Shared religious or spiritual beliefs			
Playfulness			
Mutual financial goals			
Respect for privacy			
Social activities with friends			
Gift giving and receiving			
Sharing meaningful ideas or current events			
Desire for conflict resolution			

The following two activities are opportunities to put some fun into exploring your needs and wants.

Wants and Needs Date Night

Plan a date night where each partner gets a need (must-have) and a want (like-to-have). For example, one partner could request a "need" of undivided quality time of two hours and a "want" of a picnic under the stars.

Two Truths and a Lie

Each partner takes a turn sharing three things they need in a relationship, except that one of the three is not actually true for them. In other words, two of those needs are true, while one is false. The other partner guesses which one is false, and then they discuss together why the two true needs are important to them.

If you've recently discussed your respective wants and needs charts, hopefully you'll be able to tell right away which one of your partner's stated needs is the false one!

Unifying Goals and Dreams

As humans we grow, develop, and change. Sometimes it's a subtle shift, and other times it may feel like we are a completely different person than we used to be. Sometimes we change just as individuals, and other times we evolve together as a couple.

If we change as individuals, we may be struggling with an internal battle. We might have difficulty staying true to who we are now versus who we were previously. Perhaps we don't want to tell our partner our current needs and wants, especially if they've changed, because we are afraid we will lose our partner if we do.

It's OK to change. We are supposed to. But what we can forget is that we can change together. And that starts with talking about our shared dreams as a couple. These are the things both partners want from the relationship, which might include getting married, having kids, living in a particular location, or just sharing the adventure of life together. When couples feel like they want different things, it's helpful for them to restore their shared dreams mindset by having conversations about their evolving values, goals, and dreams. These conversations are necessary in order to continue growing forward as a couple.

To make them less daunting, here are a few ways to make the conversations light and fun. Feel free to pick a few exercises or do them all if you're inspired.

Activities for Unifying Goals and Dreams

Visualizing Your Future Life Together: This game is a great way to envision your life years from now. Sit down with your partner, and each of you take some time to write down your ideal vision of your relationship in *one year*. Be specific and describe details such as where you're living, how you feel, what your day-to-day activities are, whether you have children or how they're doing, and so on. Then do the same for *five years* from now, followed by *twenty years* from now. When you're finished, take turns reading what you've written to each other. Talk about the commonalities you see as well as the differences.

Unity Vision Board: Where do you see your relationship in the future? To help flesh out your vision of your ideal future and bring it to life, create a vision board — a collage of images and words that depict your dream future. To do this, gather some magazines, scissors, glue or tape, paper, markers, and poster board, and sit down with your partner. Spend some time going through the magazines and cutting out pictures and words that depict what you each wish to see in your relationship down the road. You can also draw your own pictures or print images you find online. Then talk about the images you chose and have fun designing your vision board together by adhering them to the poster board.

Goals and Values Q&A: Ask each other the following questions to learn more about what you both envision going forward:

1. What are your top relationship goals?
2. What do you want to change about yourself in this partnership?
3. What are three things we can do to help strengthen the relationship?

> **Couples Wish List:** Together develop a list of things that you want to experience as a couple. This could include relationship goals, travel destinations, personal goals, and more.
>
> **Shared Dreams Q&A:** Another good activity to overcome differences is to explore shared dreams and visions. To do this, partners can sit down with each other and discuss the following questions:

1. What were our shared dreams together when we started our relationship?
2. What are our current shared dreams?
3. If our shared dreams haven't come to fruition, why not?
4. Can we still make those shared dreams a reality?

Our wants, needs, values, goals, and dreams are bound to differ from our partners', but we want to focus on the overlap and find solutions that work for both of us. If we can have open conversations about our wants and needs, we can have a stronger and more unified relationship.

Creating a Values Pie Chart

When couples need help determining what is important to each person in terms of their relationship, I often ask them to create a personal values pie chart. See the next page for an example.

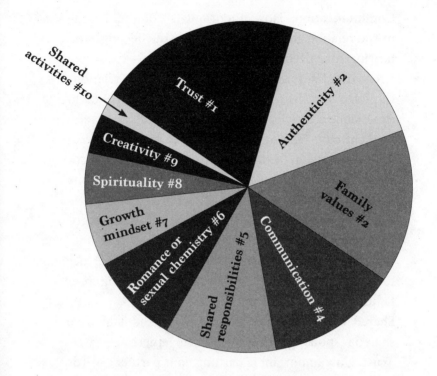

To start the chart, each partner should grab their own piece of paper and pencil (ideally with an eraser, in case you want to make adjustments as you go). The idea is that each partner will create their own chart separately and then share them afterward.

STEP 1

First, think about what is important to you in this partnership. I suggest thinking in terms of the following ten categories, but feel free to create your own or omit those that don't apply. You can also use any of the categories from the Needs and Wants chart.

- **Communication:** How important is communicating in the relationship? Are expressing your feelings and hearing your partner's concerns a priority?
- **Creativity:** How important is creativity in the relationship? Do you need your partner to be creative or to experience creativity together?
- **Authenticity:** How important is it to feel genuine in your relationship or to feel your partner is authentic?
- **Shared activities:** How important is it to like the same activities or hobbies?
- **Romance or sexual chemistry:** How important is romance or sexual chemistry in the relationship?
- **Growth mindset:** How important is it for your partner to have a growth mindset? This refers to learning from failures and wanting to grow.
- **Shared responsibilities:** How important is it to have shared responsibilities in your life together?
- **Trust:** How important is trusting your partner's words and actions?
- **Family values:** How important is it to have the same family values?
- **Spirituality:** How important is it for your partner to be spiritual or have spiritual values?

STEP 2

Once you've chosen the values that are most important for you in the relationship (both from the list above and any you've added), rank those values from 1 to 10 (or however many categories you have). In this case, 1 would be the most important value and 10 would be the least important value. If some values are equal in importance, give them the same rank, and skip the next rank in the order. The point is to determine each value's relative importance compared to the others. For example, "trust" might be number 1 for you, while "family values" and "authenticity" might both be next and equal, and so each would be number 2. Then, if "communication" was next, it would be 4, and so on.

Creating a pie chart may feel overwhelming to some. If you've gotten this far and feel like it's enough, feel free to skip ahead to step 4 and compare your lists instead of making pie charts. With that said, having the visual of the pie chart can be very helpful, so go for it if you can.

STEP 3

Next, draw a large circle for your pie chart and mark a "slice" for each value you chose. However, make the size of each slice roughly equivalent to that value's ranking. That is, the value ranked number 1 would be the biggest slice, values with the same rank would be the same size (such as if there were two values ranked at 2), and each lower-ranked value would be a smaller slice. Write the value and its ranking in each slice.

If you want to keep things simpler, make all the pie slices the same size and just write in the ranking of each value. The point is not to make the perfect chart but to help you and your partner visualize your values.

STEP 4

Once both you and your partner have finished your charts, compare and discuss them. Explain your rankings, the choices you made, and why. For example, someone might explain why "authenticity" and "family values" were tied in importance, why they were less important than "trust" and more important than other values. Partners should discuss where their values align, where they don't, and why.

Determining needs from wants, unifying goals and dreams, and creating a values pie chart are fun and unique ways to help partners communicate about what is important to them in the relationship. These exercises can also build teamwork skills, improve problem-solving abilities, and open up communication in the partnership. Ultimately, the purpose of these activities is to help partners identify shared and individual goals so they can reach them together as a unit.

ISSUE 15

"There Is Too Much Anger Between Us"

Anger is a powerful emotion. It can have a remarkable influence over our thoughts, actions, and behaviors. While it is a natural feeling and we all experience it from time to time, it can often feel uncomfortable. Contrary to its reputation, anger isn't always wrong or "bad." Anger can be helpful if we need it to push us to set boundaries, motivate us to action, or remind us of our worth. It can also help us with defending and standing up for ourselves when we experience injustice.

If not managed correctly, however, anger can have significant negative consequences. Anger can lead to physical or violent interactions, it can damage relationships, and it can negatively impact our physical and mental health. To avoid this, we need to recognize anger when it arises and then learn how to respond to it in healthy and appropriate ways. Perhaps the most helpful, important response when we feel angry is to pause. Pausing is powerful and can help save us from saying words or taking actions that cause harm, make situations worse, or lead to dire consequences. Once we pause, we can channel our anger into appropriate behaviors, like going for a walk, calling a friend, taking some deep breaths, and more. This is the function of a time-out, which I discuss in "Time-Outs" (page 19).

Then, once we are calmer, it's important to understand the deeper roots of anger, or why we felt angry over what someone

171

did or said. This chapter provides three tools for that exploration: uncovering the emotions behind anger, identifying perspectives to let go of, and empathizing with our partner.

Uncovering the Emotions Behind Anger

Anger is complex and can be triggered by a variety of factors. Anger is often called a secondary emotion because it can cover up vulnerable emotions underneath it. It may seem like anger is the star of the show with how powerful it appears, but when anger arises in a relationship, it's really the emotions behind the scenes we want to take a look at.

Here is a three-step process for identifying our emotions, taking accountability for them, and then having a conversation with our partner about how to resolve the situation and move forward.

Step 1: Identifying the Primary Emotions

To manage our anger, we need to understand it. This means uncovering the emotions that lie beneath it. These are typically one or more of five primary emotions that I like to identify with the acronym SHADE: sad, hurt, afraid, disappointed, embarrassed.

Both partners should answer the following questions on their own, which will help identify the primary emotions that may have led to anger. If we can understand the primary emotions, we can help heal the anger.

> **Sad:** If you close your eyes and think about why you are sad in the relationship, what comes up for you? Was there a loss in the relationship? Do you feel unseen or unheard in the relationship?

Hurt: When we feel hurt by something our partner has said or done, we can often respond with anger. Has your partner done something that has hurt you? Is it possible your partner may not be aware of the hurt you feel and why? If your partner has hurt you, do you need more remorse or an apology? If this is the case, see "Starting the Forgiveness Process" (page 78).

Afraid: Do you feel afraid or unsafe in the relationship, and can you pinpoint why? Are you afraid of losing your partner or of your partner ending the relationship? If there is any type of abuse, please see the resources in Issue 12: "I Don't Feel Respected by My Partner" (page 135).

Disappointed: Disappointment arises when our expectations for the relationship aren't met. Do you have an idea of how your partner should be acting but isn't? Is there a particular issue you have talked about, or an agreement made, that your partner hasn't following through on? If your partner has disappointed you, specify how.

Embarrassed: Embarrassment is a very vulnerable feeling that can lead to anger because we feel an urge to defend ourselves in order to save face. Has your partner embarrassed you in a conscious or unconscious way that has caused you to become defensive? Are you embarrassed about something you've done or caused?

Step 2: Taking Accountability

Once we identify the primary emotions behind our anger, we can then be accountable. Accountability means owning our role in the situation. We need to be accountable to both ourselves and our partner. With ourselves, that means recognizing our deeper emotions without judgment. With our partner, that means looking at how our emotions and feelings may have impacted our partner, consciously or unconsciously. We have the right to our feelings, but we don't have the right to mistreat others. It may be hard to admit our role and any harm we've caused, especially when we are initially focused on the reasons for our own anger, but repairing our relationship starts with us. We need to own our part. That means considering our actions. Have we been bitter, cold, blaming, or avoidant toward our partner?

Admitting wrongdoing shows maturity. It reminds our partners that although we've made mistakes in the relationship, we can repair them. No one is perfect, but admitting our role demonstrates the willingness to work together to be better.

Step 3: Talking with Our Partner

Once we have uncovered our emotions and taken responsibility for them, we can talk to our partner about the source of conflict and anger, the roles both persons have played, and how to fix things and move forward. If a partner doesn't feel comfortable talking about themselves, the other person can still explain their understanding and their part.

Here is one way someone might start this conversation:

> I really honor our partnership. I feel there is some anger between us, and I want to work together through it so we can have a less volatile relationship going forward. I understand it may be uncomfortable for both of us, but it's important we uncover what is really upsetting us in order to heal and rebuild. I have been doing some work

to see my part, and I'd like to share that with you. Thank you for trying to work on our relationship with me.

The person can then explain what they uncovered using SHADE. If both partners complete SHADE, then they both would share. The partners should identify what they've uncovered that they need to talk about, especially any misunderstandings that need to be cleared.

Then discuss accountability. Here is an example of taking responsibility:

After uncovering the emotion behind the anger, I've realized I've felt disappointed in your career situation. My part is that I held an unfair expectation, and at times I was cold to you because of that. I stonewalled you and belittled you. I'm truly sorry. Looking back, I thought you'd pass your law exam and immediately go into practice. I have felt disappointed that you've been out of work for two years, and I recognize I am angry because I've had to be the primary breadwinner for our family. I no longer want to be angry or cold to you. I am hopeful after talking about my feelings that we can develop a new and more balanced financial situation.

Finally, each partner should think about and explain what they need going forward. Is it an explanation or an apology? Perhaps a plan and commitment for change or action?

Here is an example of moving forward by taking action:

Perhaps we could brainstorm other ways for you to work or set up a meeting with a career counselor. If there are ways we could equalize the finances, I'd feel less pressure for the family.

Once we understand what is below the surface of anger, we can begin to have the tough but valuable conversations about why we feel the way we do. It starts, however, with examining our underlying emotions and admitting our role. Only then can we start mending and rebuilding our relationship.

Perspectives to Let Go

Letting go of anger toward a partner is a challenging process. Staying angry can make us feel like we are in control. It's the belief that if we are angry, we are dominant and have the power. There is a fear that if we are no longer angry, we no longer have the upper hand and we've let our guard down. This is an illusion and simply not true. Instead, letting go of anger allows us to change and heal our relationship. Letting go and forgiving is healthier for both partners and the relationship. Ultimately, there is more power in a loving relationship than a volatile one.

Here are some ways to let go of anger toward a partner:

1. **Write a letter to your partner about why you are angry (but don't give it to them):** The idea here is to organize your feelings without harming your partner or the relationship. The point of writing about your anger is to release the negative emotions that you have been carrying. Consider sharing the letter with a therapist if you need more processing.

2. **Question your motives:** Ask yourself honestly what you're getting by holding on to anger. Do you fear that you'll get hurt again if you forgive? Scared that if you're no longer angry you'll lose power in the relationship? Worried that if you're not angry you won't be respected? Understand the reasons it's hard to let go of being angry.

3. **Understand that forgiveness is a process:** Forgiveness is a process, not an event. That means it's OK if you haven't forgiven right away, or don't feel ready yet to forgive. But recognize there is a time to forgive and let go in order to heal the relationship.

4. **Practice a forgiveness meditation toward your partner:** There is a reason I say "practice" a forgiveness meditation, since this is simple to understand but not always easy to do. Visualize your partner and send them positive thoughts and wishes. Although it may feel like it's a gift toward them, it's actually a gift to you. You give yourself the gift of no longer carrying this emotional burden.

5. **Recite a prayer:** If prayer is something you're open to, consider reciting the Hawaiian forgiveness prayer called Ho'oponopono. It consists of four phrases: "I'm sorry. Please forgive me. Thank you. I love you." Repeat this like a mantra or chant over and over again. Similar to the forgiveness meditation, this gives yourself the gift of letting go of pain and emotions that no longer serve you or the relationship.

6. **Create a piece of art:** Being creative artistically can help us process emotions. Draw, paint, or color a picture of yourself forgiving your partner or of anything else that symbolizes letting go.

7. **Make a commitment to be less angry:** Have the intention to be less angry toward your partner. This could be a general commitment or something specific you pledge to do, like take time each day to appreciate your partner for who they are and what they've done. You might remind yourself of the steps you both are taking to rebuild the relationship and be more connected moving forward.

8. **Create a goodbye ritual:** Write down your anger on a piece of paper and crumple it up. Either bury the paper in the ground or burn it in a ceremonial fire. The idea is to acknowledge your anger while also letting it go.

9. **List your partner's positive qualities:** Write down a list of your partner's best qualities. Thinking about the positive can help shift us out of anger.

10. **Be cognizant of false assumptions and stories:** Our imaginations can sometimes make inaccurate assumptions or create false stories about how our partners feel, what they will say, or other negative actions they might take. These are often based on our fears and emotions, not on the other person. We can remind ourselves that we may be creating a false narrative, and instead of assuming, we can ask our partner how they feel.

Letting go of anger takes time and effort. But if we make efforts to actively release anger, we can start cultivating a healthier and more positive relationship with our partner.

Empathizing with Our Partner

Cruz and Elea were a couple in their forties who had "a lot of anger" between them. I sensed this when they came into my office. The two sat as far away as possible on my couch and turned their heads in opposite directions. You could cut the tension with a knife.

Each felt like the victim in their situation. Cruz told me he was upset because Elea was out all night "clubbing" with her friends while he worked. He said he felt angry because he was working the late shift while Elea was partying.

Elea told me she was angry with Cruz because he was

working "all the time." She said she felt angry because she didn't feel like a priority, and her friends were always there for her.

This had created a negative cycle. The more Cruz worked, the more Elea went out. The more Elea went out, the more Cruz felt upset. The more they both avoided each other, the more anger developed.

I asked Elea, "What do you think Cruz is feeling when you go out clubbing?"

Elea looked a bit annoyed at the thought. "Um, I think he's angry."

"OK," I said, "but what else?"

She thought for a moment. "I think he's hurt because I'm not including him when I go out."

I turned to Cruz. "Is she right?"

Cruz put his head down and nodded. "I am hurt. I want to be with you, too. I know I'm working a lot, but even when I'm not, it's like you don't want to be with me."

"Cruz," I said, "what about you? What do you think Elea is feeling when you are working all the time?"

"I'm going to guess lonely?" he questioned.

"Elea?" I asked.

"Yes," she said. "If you were around more or made our date nights a bigger deal, I think I'd go out with my friends less."

In that moment, Cruz and Elea experienced a perspective shift. They turned their heads toward each other like they were finally seeing each other after all this time. They recognized they both wanted the same thing, to be with each other.

My questions helped Cruz and Elea feel empathy with each other. They understood each other's feelings. This is important because, when we are angry, we can get self-righteous and think our point of view is the only point of view. We forget to consider the feelings and perspective of others.

Once Elea and Cruz could empathize with what the other was feeling and see from their perspective, this transformed their anger into understanding.

I pointed out the obvious — that they both wanted to see more of each other. We worked on Elea and Cruz being more communicative about what they needed; I also had them schedule date nights. Cruz switched to working more day shifts, and he made Elea a priority on their scheduled date nights.

If we can empathize with our partner, we can understand why they are upset. During an argument, I encourage partners to pause and check in with how they are each feeling. One person can ask the other, "What do you think I'm feeling right now?" Then they can switch. This can help both partners shift their perspectives on the situation.

Empathy is a skill that improves with practice. Over time, practicing empathy with our partner enables us to see and appreciate their feelings and point of view.

Anger is natural reaction and it occurs in all relationships. It's how we manage anger that makes all the difference. This involves identifying the emotions beneath our anger, making an effort to let go of anger, and empathizing with our partner to understand their point of view.

Conclusion

The things we value often take time, commitment, and work. Our relationships are no different. My goal has been to create a couples relationship book with "love hacks" that are accessible, encouraging, and easy for couples to utilize. That is my part. Your part is to implement the tools and exercises to repair and improve your relationship. That part is much harder, more uncomfortable, and takes legitimate effort. To get honest, be vulnerable, and sit in discomfort is not easy. Whether you are working along with your partner or on your own, I applaud you for working to improve your relationship. It is an achievement simply to take the time and effort to prioritize your partnership in the midst of so many other responsibilities and obligations. By reading this book and incorporating the exercises and activities, you are honoring and valuing your relationship.

It's normal for relationships to ebb and flow. There are certain times when we feel more connected to our partner than others. All relationships can experience fallings-out, misunderstandings, and lack of connection at times. But if we take the care and time to improve, things can fall back into place.

There is growth in overcoming obstacles. Experiencing hardships with a partner can teach us lessons that improve the partnership. We can learn what works and what doesn't work.

We can recognize the value in painful experiences, approaching them as tools that teach us and guide us in new directions.

Always remember that work on a partnership includes our own personal development, since it requires learning more about ourselves and understanding our strengths and weaknesses. This growth improves us as individuals even as it helps our partnership. Whatever happens in a relationship, we can always ask ourselves: Who do *we* want to be in this relationship?

Thank you for being courageous to seek help and thank you for trusting me for insights and guidance. Revisit these tools at any time. They can help you and your relationship improve, one love hack at a time.

Acknowledgments

Thank you first and foremost to my literary agent, Linda Konner, who reached out to me after reading my advice column in 2009. Since then, Linda, you never stopped believing in me. I'm so grateful for your help in making my dreams come true. I love both your New York honesty and your accent.

Speaking of dreams, thank you to Georgia Hughes, my editor. You have the perfect combination of being gentle but effective with your edits and suggestions. You saw this book's future and were confident in my abilities from the start.

Thank you to everyone at New World Library for allowing me to be part of all the great books that have made differences in people's lives. A special thank-you to Jeff Campbell for your rock-star grammatical edits; Kristen Cashman for your sincere and stellar dedication to this book and your extraordinarily helpful edits; Tanya Fox for your incredible last-minute catches; Tracy Cunningham for your gorgeous artistic eye and creating the perfect cover; Tona Pearce Myers for creating the perfect interior design for the book; and Monique Muhlenkamp for taking it all home with the wonderful publicity help.

Thank you to my parents, Candi and Alan, whose marriage helped inspire this book. You've weathered the storms and showed true commitment. Mom, you continue to be the best support I have. I love that I can call you seven times a day. Dad, your logic and business skills helped develop my career. And I credit you for teaching me how to become a better writer. I love you both beyond words.

Thank you, Remy and London, my two boys. Remy, your heart is, and always has been, one of the kindest that I know. I love your gentle nature and ability to always be sensitive to others. London, you have been, and still are, one of the most charming and magnetic children I've ever seen. We have so much fun when we are together. I'm a lucky mom to have the two of you. I love you both to the moon and back.

To all my therapist friends and colleagues: You've made me a better, more insightful, and wiser therapist. Without you, I'm not sure I'd be as professionally and personally happy. Thank you for your continued support.

To my dear friends (you know who you are): I'm not sure where I'd be without your love, laughter, and loyalty. I recognize every single day how lucky I am to have you.

To all my past, current, and future couples clients, thank you for putting your trust in me to help your relationship. I love what I do and feel honored to get the opportunity to help you as well as others.

Notes

p. 43　*This description of sensate focus therapy is based*: William Masters, Virginia Johnson, and Robert Kolodny, *Heterosexuality* (New York: HarperCollins Perennial, 1995); and "Sensate Focus," *Cornell Health* (October 18, 2019), https://health.cornell.edu/sites/health/files/pdf-library/sensate-focus.pdf.

p. 59　*Author Jonathan Haidt made a similar point in his book*: Jonathan Haidt, *The Happiness Hypothesis* (New York: Basic Books, 2006).

p. 64　*The philosophy is based on Gary Chapman's book*: Gary Chapman, *The 5 Love Languages: The Secret to Love That Lasts* (Chicago: Northfield Publishing, 2010).

p. 67　*If you want to help discover your love language*: "The Love Language Quiz," 5 Love Languages, https://5lovelanguages.com/quizzes/love-language.

p. 83　*A helpful concept for understanding grief is Elisabeth Kübler-Ross's*: Elisabeth Kübler-Ross and David Kessler, *On Grief & Grieving: Finding the Meaning of Grief Through the Five Stages of Loss* (New York: Scribner, 2005/2014).

p. 113　*Studies have identified multiple genes associated with addiction*: Maia Szalavitz, "Genetics: No More Addictive Personality," *Nature* 522, no. 7557 (June 25, 2015); and L. Bevilacqua and D. Goldman, "Genes and Addictions," *Clinical Pharmacology and Therapeutics* 85, no. 4 (April 2009), 359–61.

About the Author

Kelli Miller, LCSW, MSW, is a psychotherapist, bestselling author, and TV/radio host. Kelli is the award-winning and bestselling author of *Thriving with ADHD Workbook for Kids*, which has been translated into multiple languages. She is a brand ambassador, writer, and relationship host for wikiHow .com, which has an estimated viewership of over 116 million monthly users. Kelli was a cohost on LA Talk Radio with over one million listeners and 250 guest celebrities and authors, was an expert radio personality for SiriusXM, and hosted a live stream called *All Things Relationships* by Balance by Nature. She was the "Women's Relationship Expert" on Examiner.com and also the advice columnist to the largest Listserv in the country. She was a freelance writer for over twelve magazines and publications, and her expertise has been quoted in various publications, including *O, The Oprah Magazine, Authority Magazine, Wellness Magazine, The Georgetown Current, The Northwest Current,* and *Now It's Your Turn Mom!*

Kelli has conducted seminars on relationships, work/life balance, and managing stress for the Westfield Mall Corporation, Los Angeles Airport (LAX), Los Angeles World Airports (LAWA), various law firms, and more. She has been a relationship expert panelist for CalState Northridge's television show and has appeared on CBS local news, the Maddox podcast *The Best Debate in the Universe, The Joe Show, Deal With It!,* and many other media outlets. She is also an adviser for Cognitive Leap's app for ADHD as well as a spokesperson for Brillia.

Kelli currently works in private practice with individuals and couples. Visit her on her website (KelliMillerTherapy.com) and on Instagram (@kellimillertherapy).

Kelli is a lover of all animals and cannot see a dog without petting it. She also loves hiking and traveling, and she's always open to a deep and reflective conversation. If you want to get on her good side, buy her some 85-percent dark chocolate.